Collins

need to know?

Bass
guitar

Paul Scott

Collins

First published in 2008 by Collins
an imprint of
HarperCollins Publishers
77–85 Fulham Palace Road
London W6 8JB

www.collins.co.uk

Collins is a registered trademark of
HarperCollins Publishers Limited

10 09 08
6 5 4 3 2 1

Text © Paul Scott, 2008

A catalogue record for this book is available from
the British Library

Editor: Rosalyn Thiro
Packager: Thameside Media Projects
Series design: Mark Thomson
Photographer: Michael Ellis
Front cover photograph: © S.I.N. / Alamy
Back cover photographs: © iStockPhoto.com

ISBN-13: 978-0-00-726114-7
ISBN-10: 0-00-726114-4

Printed and bound by Printing Express Ltd,
Hong Kong

Contents

Why play the bass guitar?

There are many reasons to play the bass guitar. To paraphrase Shakespeare, some people are born to play bass, some grow to love it, and some have it thrust upon them.

The author's experience

As a child, I always wanted to play 'the big thing at the back of the orchestra' – the double bass, in other words. I was lucky because my school offered free lessons on the double bass. You might have thought that there would have been a queue around the block, but I was the only one who lasted the course. Some of the other bass students seemed to regard the f-holes on a double bass as handy receptacles for orange peel, and no more. One day, one of the bass teachers brought in his Fender® Precision bass guitar for me to try out. I was already hooked on the double bass, and adding the bass guitar to my repertoire was just perfect. That would have been in 1970, or thereabouts, and the Precision bass guitar, or something very like it, has been one of my weapons of choice ever since.

The art of bass

So why should *you* play the bass guitar? Well, I can't tell if you and the bass guitar are a perfect match, but I can give you a few hints. Like most people who find themselves playing the bass guitar, you are probably already drawn to the sound and look of bass instruments generally, and the low frequencies on your favourite recordings. You might be drawn by

The author, Paul Scott, with his customized Yamaha BB1200 bass

the notion that the bass player is the band member who really controls the show – that basslines are the foundation of music in terms of rhythm.

You might also think that the bass guitar is a relatively simple way to start playing music. In this you would be right, in the sense that most bass guitars have only four strings, and you can start playing simple riffs (repeated phrases) quite readily.

Every bass player, of any standing, will tell you that it's the simple, basic stuff that usually gets the job done. Time and note choice, tone and note length, keeping the basic groove or swing of a piece consistent from start to finish is what the bass player's role is mostly about.

If that is what you want to do, whatever age you are, then this book will give you a good grounding in the art of playing bass guitar. Throughout the book, I mention great bass players and pieces of music that you should listen to for inspiration. The beauty of the bass guitar is that during its relatively short history it has acquired many virtuoso voices: Paul Chambers, James Jamerson, Charles Mingus, Carol Kaye, Jack Bruce, Jaco Pastorius, Jack Bruce, Jeff Berlin, Colin Hodgkinson, Robbie Shakespeare, Chris Squire, Stanley Clarke, Victor Bailey, Arthur Barrow, Flea and many others – the list grows every year. And if you are puzzled by some of the names in the list above, well... that was deliberate. Now it is up to you to find out who they are and what they have done on the bass.

Happy playing.

How to use this book

Within this book are a variety of visual cues and diagrams to help you learn how to play music with the bass guitar. We've included diagrams of the neck of the bass guitar, notation and tablature, along with left-hand fingerings.

Track 41

CD track tie-ins

The CD that comes with this book has 99 tracks that tie in with the examples and exercises throughout this book. The Track icon shows which track number on the CD relates to the page you are on.

Neck diagrams

The neck diagrams in Chapter 5 represent part of the neck of a bass and are primarily for beginners learning the shape of scales.

As on a real bass, the E string (lowest in pitch) is the thickest string, and the G string (highest in pitch) is the thinnest. However, note that the diagram looks like it's upside-down, with the order of strings reversed. This is because it reflects the way you see

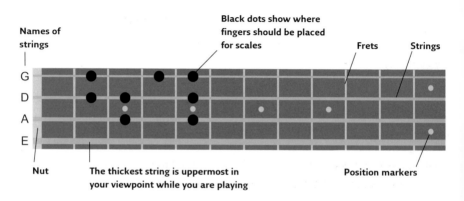

Names of strings

Black dots show where fingers should be placed for scales

Frets

Strings

G
D
A
E

Nut

The thickest string is uppermost in your viewpoint while you are playing

Position markers

and relate to the neck while actually playing, not as if looking face-on. The white dots echo the position markers on a real bass; the thick vertical line on the left is the nut; and the thin vertical lines are the frets (see pages 14–15 for more about the named parts). The black dots indicate where you should place your fingers.

For more about the neck diagrams, see page 55.

Notation

In conventional music notation, the pitches and rhythms of notes are marked on a five-line grid called the stave, shown in the upper half of the diagram below. Information about reading notation is in Chapter 4.

The row of numbers below the notation shows you which fingers to use on your left hand – 1 means first finger, 2 means second finger, and so on. For more about fingering and hand position, see page 34.

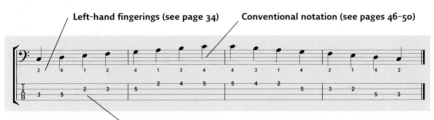

Tablature showing fret positions (see pages 50–1)

Tablature

The four-line grid in the lower half of the diagram is called tablature (TAB). Its layout is like the neck diagrams: that is, for a four-string bass the four lines represent E at the bottom, through A and D, to G at the top. The numbers suggest which frets to use on the bass guitar when playing the notes shown in the notation above. For more about tablature see pages 50–1.

1 Bass basics

The purpose of this section of the book is to
give you some background about your chosen
instrument. You will find out what the various
parts of the bass guitar are called, be given a
potted history of the instrument, and also a
description of what it actually does in a band.

What is the bass guitar?

If you have picked up this book, then you probably have a fair idea of how the bass guitar sounds, and you know that it is different from the acoustic and other electric guitars. On the whole, this book deals with the modern electric bass guitar, but also refers to related instruments, such as the double bass.

must know

In music, 'bass' simply means the lowest frequency part of a harmonic piece of music. It relates to the Italian word 'basso', meaning low, and is also derived from the Latin 'bassus', meaning base or foundation.

Terminology and context

Nowadays, the terms 'electric bass guitar', 'bass guitar', 'electric bass' or simply just 'bass' are used almost synonymously. Though potentially confusing, this helps to differentiate the instrument from other guitars. While shaped like the guitar, the bass guitar actually has a totally different lineage and history, and is in fact mostly derived from the double bass *(see pages 16–17)*.

Since the 1950s, the electric bass has mostly taken over from the double bass in popular music, providing low-pitched basslines alongside other instruments in bands. It is also played solo in various styles.

Foundation of the band

In a band, the role of the bass player, musically, is to give harmonic and rhythmic support to the rest of the band. In order to perform this role, it is very important for the bassist to understand harmony. Practising the scales, triads and arpeggios in this book *(see chapter 5)* will help you understand bass theory, as well as develop your playing skills. Following on from the basics, you can start jamming with your friends and, quite possibly, form or join a band and start to play some gigs.

It is especially important for the bassist and drummer in a band to work closely. Try out as many styles as you can together. That is, play short grooves in different styles – rock 'n'roll, reggae, punk, heavy metal etc – and learn to 'lock in' with the drums.

Whether or not you are in a band, you can practise rhythm with an electronic metronome and/or drum loops on a computer.

As well as being the musical foundation of a band, for some reason the bass player often also finds that he or she has the natural skills to be the band's organiser and arranger. For tips about joining a band and playing gigs, see pages 178–81.

see pages 178–81.

must know
The bass player provides the foundation of harmony and rhythm for the band. Harmony is acheived when all the players are using notes that sound pleasing to the ear, which is why this book places a lot of emphasis on scales.

More reasons to choose bass

With just four strings (usually), the bass guitar can be a simple instrument to start off on. You can quite quickly begin to play lines and riffs (repeated phrases) that will underpin some of your favourite songs. Once you have mastered the bass guitar, you could move on to the venerable double bass *(see pages 17 and 177)*, which is used in classical orchestras and a variety of other genres, and offers a potentially more characterful bassline.

Lifestyle aspirations can lie behind the choice of bass. The bass guitar will open up ideas about motivation and discipline: the more work that you put into any instrument, the better it gets. You could learn to play, learn to teach the instrument, become an academic, become a rock 'n' roll icon, be a great jazz improviser – even travel the world with your band.

So, what is the bass guitar? It is the coolest instrument in any band and it could be your key to a new life.

The typical four-piece band with bass guitar, guitar, singer and drums

Bass parts and related terms

Amplifier A device which converts the signal from your bass into sound via a loudspeaker (p.24).

Bridge Strings pass over the bridge to a tailpiece. The bridge assembly is either in one piece or as separates.

Fender bass Trademark of Fender® (p.18). Originally the generic term for any electric bass guitar.

Fingerboard Usually of rosewood, ebony or maple. This is where contact is made by the fingers pressing down on the strings.

Fingerstyle Plucking the strings with your fingertips (p.36).

Frets (wire) Raised strips across the neck of the bass, indicating where notes should be played. Usually made from brass and nickel, but called nickel/silver. Each fret represents one semitone (half-step interval). They are counted down from the headstock on the bass, and 21 is a common total. Some basses do not have any frets.

Headstock Where the strings are usually attached to the machine heads.

Jack socket Connection for signal from bass to amplifier.

Jazz bass (J-bass) Trademark of Fender® for the model with two separate, single-coil pickups. Is often used as a generic term (p.19).

Luthier Someone who builds and repairs guitars and basses.

Machine head Mechanism for raising or lowering the pitch of strings in tuning.

Metronome Device giving tempo.

Neck Long part of the bass where most notes are played.

Neck diagram A diagram showing where fingers go on the neck (Chapter 5).

Notation Usually a stave with notes placed on it (p.46).

Nut Place where the strings sit at the top of the neck. Ebony, bone, brass or plastic.

Octave Interval between two notes of the same name, which sound harmonically equivalent to the human ear.

Open string A string which is allowed to vibrate between the note and the bridge.

Pick/plectrum Plastic, metal or tortoiseshell; used for plucking a string (p.38).

Pickup Device that converts the vibrations from the bass into an electric signal. Basses have one or two pickups.

Pitch Frequency of a note.

Position (fret) markers Dots on the bass neck that help you find the right fret.

Single dots appear before the 3rd, 5th, 7th, 9th, 15th, 17th and 19th frets. A pair of dots marks the octave at the 12th.

Scales Sequences of notes stepping up and down like a ladder (Chapter 5).

Scratchplate A piece of plastic to protect the body from scratches.

Slapping Playing technique on bass (p.40).

Stopped note When you use your finger on a string against the fingerboard to create a note.

Strings Usually stainless steel or nickel/steel on a bass guitar, although other metals and coatings are used.

Tablature Diagrams for beginners (p.50).

Tempo Speed of the music.

Thumb rest Somewhere to rest your thumb, should you need it.

Tone knob Can be used to alter tone, usually by turning off to fatten the sound.

Truss rod A metal rod inside the neck (p.29).

Tuner Electronic device for tuning your instrument to a reference pitch or note (p.26).

Tuning post Where the end of the string goes into and is then wrapped around.

Volume knob Usually left fully open or up.

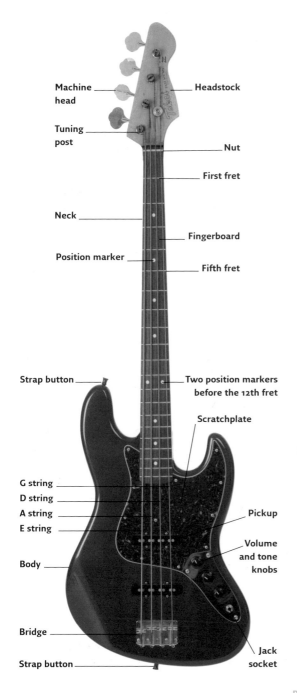

Machine head

Headstock

Tuning post

Nut

First fret

Neck

Fingerboard

Position marker

Fifth fret

Strap button

Two position markers before the 12th fret

Scratchplate

G string
D string
A string
E string

Pickup

Volume and tone knobs

Body

Bridge

Strap button

Jack socket

must know

Terminology relating to music notation, including the names of the notes, can be found on pages 46-51. You can also refer to the glossary on pages 182-5 if you ever need reminding about the meaning of any terms used in this book.

The story of the bass

A relatively young instrument in music history, the bass guitar can be thought to have two main lines of development: one from the lute or guitar, and the other from the bass viol.

The lute is a cousin of the bass guitar

Bass version of the lute

Both the lute and guitar are descended from the Arabic *oud*, which was brought to Spain by the Moors during their occupation of the Iberian peninsula from 711 to 1492. The long-necked bass version of the lute is called the *theorbo* (or, in Italian, *chittarone*). It was popular during the 17th and 18th centuries as an accompanying instrument, and some solo music was written for it in tablature. The *theorbo* is still played in some authentic Baroque ensembles as part of the *basso continuo*, a term also known as 'thoroughbass' or 'figured bass', which refers to the harmonic structure provided by bass notes.

Acoustic bass developments

Different types of acoustic basses emerged in the mid-20th century. In the 1930s companies such as Gibson, Dobro and Regal produced various large-bodied bass instruments. Gibson created the mandobass to provide the bottom end for mandolin orchestras. Such orchestras were popular at the time, although the mandobass itself never really took off. To listen to a related instrument, check out Weather Report's *Heavy Weather* album (1971), in which bass player Jaco Pastorius plays the mandocello on *Birdland*.

Gibson also developed an upright electric bass guitar with a single electrical pickup, which was used in guitarist Les Paul's trio in the 1940s.

In a separate situation, Mexican mariachi bands have long used the guitarron as a bass instrument, from which Ernie Ball developed an acoustic bass guitar in the early 1970s.

The bass viol

The bass viol, or violone, started life in the Renaissance era as a six-stringed instrument with tied gut frets to help with intonation. The author of this book owns a double bass that started life in the 18th century as a three-stringed bass viol, and which had a fourth string added at some point in the 19th or early 20th century. In the 21st century it has been given some cast-bronze, high-geared tuning devices.

Companies such as Rickenbacker made the Electro bass-viol in 1936. This was a double bass neck with a pickup and an amplifier. Regal and Vega also made similar instruments.

The double bass

Descended from the bass viol, the double bass is also known as the upright bass, acoustic bass, string base or contrabass. Like the electric bass guitar, it is also referred to simply as 'the bass'. This instrument remains popular in a variety of genres, such as symphony orchestras, but it is its use in jazz ensembles from the mid-20th century onwards that has given it its highest profile.

There are many comparisons to be drawn between the bass guitar and double bass, even though the two instruments look so different. In general, the

The double bass was adopted by music ensembles in New Orleans in the early 20th century, and its usage was widespread in jazz bands by the 1940s

bass guitar is often the most versatile instrument for a variety of situations, but the double bass can certainly provide a greater palette of tonal colours. Artists such as Stanley Clarke and Christian McBride are creative on both instruments, and all bass players can gain inspiration by listening to the double bass. For this reason we have included the great double bassists Charles Mingus and Paul Chambers later in this book.

Birth of the Fender bass

In 1951, the American instrument maker Leo Fender launched a new type of electric stringed instrument – the Precision bass. Shaped like a guitar, this instrument was considerably smaller than the acoustic double bass that was widely used in jazz clubs at the time. His motives were partly to help bass players overcome problems in transporting huge double basses, partly to amplify the bass sound easily through an amplifier, and also partly to appeal to rhythm or lead guitarists who might be looking to double on bass.

The American company Fender® makes a wide range of stringed instruments and amplifiers, and has been the industry standard for bass guitars since the 1950s.

The original Precision bass had a 34in. scale string length similar to that of a guitar. In fact, the Precision was based on the appearance of Fender's earlier Telecaster electric guitar, and had a maple neck bolted onto an ash body, with a single coil electrical pickup. It was called the Precision because the frets made it easier than the fretless double bass to play notes in tune.

Leo Fender made the Precision's body more streamlined in 1954, with the introduction of contours similar to the newly built Stratocaster guitar. Then, in 1957, a new split, 'humbucking' pickup was added to the bass, and this remains the basic design of the Precision bass today.

In 1960, Leo Fender brought out a new bass guitar design, the Fender® Jazz bass. This instrument was narrower at the nut than the Precision bass, with a more heavily contoured body and two single coil pickups. It wasn't necessarily used primarily for jazz. The slim neck was a godsend for players with smaller hands, or guitarists who wanted to play bass.

The Precision (P-bass) and the Jazz (J-bass) are the accepted basis for most bass guitar designs today.

Rickenbacker and Gibson

Rickenbacker have been building some excellent basses since the late 50s. Their 4001S model, which Paul McCartney started to play in 1965, became a much sought-after instrument during the early 70s by some of the progressive rock players. Chris Squire of Yes also had his Rickenbacker from 1965.

Gibson have continued to make some excellent models over the years, too – John Entwistle's love of the Thunderbird is well documented.

want to know more?
• For more about the history of the bass guitar, read: How The Fender Bass Changed The World by Jim Roberts (2001, Backbeat)
• The Bass Book: A Complete Illustrated History Of Bass Guitars by Tony Bacon & Barry Moorhouse (2005, Backbeat)
• The Fender Bass by Klaus Blasquiz (1991, Music Sales)
• The Fender Bass: An Illustrated History, by J.W.Black (2001, Hal Leonard)

weblinks
• www.fender.com for the official Fender site
• www.basscentre.com is a major specialist
• www.thebassgallery.com is a great outlet in London

2 Your bass guitar

In this chapter we will look at what kind of bass guitar to choose. Also, we will guide you to the right amplifier for practice and gigging. As well as this, there is guidance on how to tune your instrument, and also a section on how to maintain your bass in peak condition.

Choosing an instrument

Look at basses that feel good and also sound good. Then go away and think about it. Try not to buy on impulse. Take time with a purchase, and the same bass could last you for years.

must know

It is possible to have a custom bass built to your own specifications. See the webography on page 189 for a few of the best builders, who are called luthiers.

Finding the right size

The first thing you need to consider is your own hand size. For those players with larger hands then either a long scale 34in. (86cm) Precision (P-bass) or Jazz-style (J-bass) would be the best option. Decide if you need the strings at the nut closer or further apart. Beginners with larger hands who need a bit more room to dig in should go for a P-bass spacing at the nut (42mm). For those who like a slimmer neck, then a J-bass spacing would be more appropriate (38mm).

For those beginners with much smaller hands, Squier make a short-scale 30in. (76cm) bass called the Bronco, which is based on the old Fender Mustang-type of bass. It has a 38mm width nut, the same as the J-bass, but the shorter string length makes it easier to play. (Anyone thinking this is a soft option should listen to Deep Purple's *Fireball* album; Roger Glover is playing a Mustang on that recording.)

The question of cost

The cost of your first instrument is always a major factor for a beginner. Shop around both physically and also on the Internet, and look at secondhand as well as new instruments. The first port of call should be a large music store – but don't take your credit card on the first visit. Also check the small print of online deals before you commit to buying.

From front to back: a Yamaha®
four-string BB1200, a Fender® Jazz
bass, a MusicMan® five-string bass
and a Tokai four-string bass

Amplification

You're not going to get far on a bass guitar without an amplifier and speaker. Usually, the combination (or combo), is a good style to go for. That is, the amplifier and speaker come in one box, which is easier than separates to transport.

The question of size

Usually the best approach is to use the smallest bass amp that will do the job. If you find yourself touring with a band that has roadies, then feel free to get the largest Ampeg, Ashdown, MesaBoogie or Marshall rig that your pocket can afford. For the rest of us, who have to carry our own gear, then portability and compact size are the keys to any amplifier purchase.

The best speaker size for bass is a 15in. (38cm), followed by a combination of 10in. (25cm) speakers and, sometimes, a 12in. (30cm) speaker. The author has a couple of small amplifiers that can be used with different speakers. This can also be a good option for getting the amplifier into, and out of, venues.

A small SWR 'Baby Baby Blue' combo and a medium-sized Hughes & Kettner combo

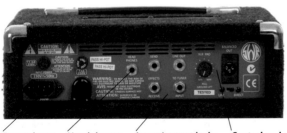

Front panel of the SWR 'Baby Baby Blue'

| Input jacks | Pre-amp booster for extra volume | Equalization controls for bass, treble, etc | Control for 'dry/wet' sound effects | Master volume control | On/off switch |

Back panel of the SWR 'Baby Baby Blue'

| Power input | Headphones jack | Input/output jacks for tuner and other equipment | Control and output to a mixing console |

Manufacturers

The companies mentioned opposite offer good ranges. There are also many other manufacturers that make small combos. Some of the quality ones that spring readily to mind are SWR, Mark, Hughes & Kettner, Warwick, Hartke and Fender®.

Several small amplifiers are dedicated for double bass usage, such as Acoustic Image, Euphonic Audio, Gallien Krueger Microbass – and Polytone, which can be used with both bass guitar and double bass.

Cable for connecting a bass to an amp

Tuning and intonation

Tuning is the process by which you adjust the pitch of your instrument so that it is identical to a reference pitch. This is often done using an electronic tuner, but other devices can be used. You should check if your bass is in tune each time you use it.

The pitch of a string is altered by twisting the machine head clockwise (to loosen and decrease pitch) or anti-clockwise (to tighten and increase pitch) until the sound of the open string matches that of the reference pitch.

How to use the tuning track

Tuning a bass is best done to the open strings, starting with the G string. In other words, you play the full-length string without 'stopping' it anywhere on the fingerboard, while adjusting the machine head until the pitch of the string is tuned.

Track 1 of the CD plays the four open strings of the bass guitar to give you a reference for tuning. Each open string – GDAE – is sounded four times.

Other devices and methods

You may not always have access to this CD when you are playing or performing, so at some point you will probably want to buy a separate tuning device that will plug straight into your bass guitar. Stroboscopic tuning devices, which use strobe light frequency to match pitch, are very accurate, but there are many cheaper tuners on the market that also do a good job.

A high-quality tuner, such as this electronic Korg tuner, has open string settings and a dial that shows you at a glance if the pitch of a string is sharp or flat.

It is also possible to tune to a piano. Play the G on the piano at the same time as the G on the bass so that the notes resonate, and adjust the string until the notes sound clear together.

Some bass players will also check the pitch of an open string against the identical stopped note on the fifth fret of the string below. Alternatively, you can tune using the harmonics – the harmonic at the seventh fret of the G string will be identical to the harmonic at the fifth fret of the D string.

Checking intonation

Intonation is a word that can be used to describe two separate, but related, things. Firstly, if an instrument like a violin, fretless bass guitar or clarinet is in tune relative to a tuning note but is being played slightly out of tune by the player, then that person's intonation can be said to be faulty. Secondly, due to the physics of different string metals, instrument woods and string lengths used on guitars and bass guitars, the pitch of the stopped note at the twelfth fret may be out of tune with the harmonic at the twelfth fret, or even out of tune with the open string. It is then that the bridge can be adjusted, backwards or forwards, so that this stopped note (and all others) is in tune with the open string.

To check intonation after you have tuned the four open strings, place your finger at the twelfth fret and play the note. Depending on whether this note is sharp or flat *(see glossary)*, you then need to move the bridge saddle up or down, usually with the aid of a Phillips (cross-shaped) screwdriver. Whether you have to screw clockwise or anti-clockwise to find the right intonation is a matter of trial and error.

Track 1

The tuning track on the CD repeats each note on the open strings – GDAE.

The bridge saddle is adjusted with a screwdriver.

Maintenance

Routine maintenance for a bass includes cleaning and oiling the wood, and changing strings that have dulled over time. Repairs to any damaged parts are usually best left to experts.

Cleaning

It is necessary to keep the body, neck and fingerboard of your bass clean. It is best to use proprietary guitar cleaner and a lint-free cloth. Try not to use general household cleaning products, some of which can contain silicone and wax.

The fingerboard of your instrument can be cleaned with a light alcohol such as surgical spirit or isopropyl alcohol. Unfortunately, the alcohol removes water as

Remove grease and smudges from the body of your bass by rubbing with a lint-free cloth.

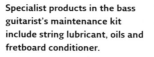

Specialist products in the bass guitarist's maintenance kit include string lubricant, oils and fretboard conditioner.

well as dirt from unvarnished wood. Therefore you should regularly rub the fingerboard with lemon oil to stop the wood from drying out.

Changing strings

It's a good idea to change your strings when they have lost their brilliance, unless you actually like a dull, thuddy tone with no sustain. The author of this book has a rule (albeit non-scientific) that every set of strings only has so many notes in it: when you've used up all of those notes, then change your strings.

You can take off the strings one, or two, at a time, starting with the thinnest string. This presents a good opportunity to clean the fingerboard with a few drops of lemon oil applied using a cotton wool pad. Once the new string has been passed through the bridge, then over the bridge and straight over the nut, measure about a finger's length from the tuning post along the string. Any excess at the end of the string can then be snipped off with a pair of wire cutters. This prevents having too much excess string wrapped around the barrels of the tuners.

Place the end of the string into the hole in the middle of the post, and wind it so that it goes from top to bottom. This will keep the string firmly in place at the nut.

Truss rod adjustment

The truss rod is a metal rod inside the neck of a bass that stops the neck from bowing because of the tension in the strings. A lot of bass players adjust this themselves with confidence, but beginners are best advised to leave this to a specialist craftsperson to get the job done safely.

Always have spare packets of strings to hand.

want to know more?
• Minor problems with leads and jack sockets can sometimes be fixed with simple soldering, but use a dedicated electronic soldering iron and lead-free solder
• For more on maintenance, check Bass Guitar Care And Setup: FAQ by John LeVan (2005, Mel Bay)

weblinks
If you are buying a bass, check these websites:
• www.fender.com
• basscentre.com
• thebassgallery.com
• guitaremporium.co.uk
• guitar-xperience.com
• overwater.co.uk
• wildguitars.com

3 Getting started

In this section, we will demonstrate comfortable and correct hand positions for playing, while sitting down and while standing. There are three short sections on fingerstyle, playing with a plectrum, and slap technique on the bass. As well as this, we have given you two tried and tested warm-up exercises to get your hands and muscles working.

Comfortable posture

There are a few tips on posture that should help you as you start playing the bass guitar. The way you hold the instrument will affect the way that you play it in the long term.

The author shows a new student how to adopt a comfortable hand position on the neck of the bass guitar. This was the student's first lesson on the instrument.

Height of play

First of all, the strap should be set at a length so that the bass sits mid-chest in height. Some players have the bass set too high, which constricts the right hand and can cause problems in the wrist of the right hand. Conversely, some players will set the bass much too low, even having the bass hanging around the knees. While this might look cool for playing live with a punk band, it makes it very difficult to use a comfortable left-hand fingering.

Once the strap height is set, then the bass should be in the same position on your body whether you are sitting down or standing up (see opposite).

Weight of instrument

Sometimes, you might wish to remove the strap to give your own neck a rest from the pressure of having a heavy piece of wood hanging around it. Be aware that, should you do so, you will have to use the left (or fingering) hand to hold up the neck of the bass while also fingering the notes with the same hand. This will slow down your playing.

One way of getting around the heavy weight of the bass on your own neck is to use an elastic strap. There are several different types on the market and they do work. Stiff leather straps will usually bite into your neck after a short time of playing. However, the main point is that you should use an adjustable strap that is comfortable for you. (The author uses elastic straps on all of his bass guitars.)

When playing in a standing position, make sure the strap on the bass guitar is set to a height so that you can reach any position on the neck of the instrument comfortably.

You should still wear a strap when playing in a sitting position. Make sure that the strap genuinely supports the bass guitar so that your hands can play easily and do not have to grip the instrument.

Hand and finger positioning

To follow the music in this book, you need to understand the fingering numbers for the left hand, which are written below the musical notes in most examples throughout the book. You also need to know about the most comfortable hand positions to use.

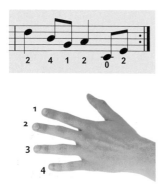

o = open string (no fingering)

Fingering guidance for the left hand is shown as a row of numbers below the notes. The music sample above indicates that the first note is to be played with finger 2; the second note with finger 4; the third note with finger 1, and so on.

Fingering guidance

Most examples in this book have numbers below the notes showing which finger of your left hand is best to use, as in the sample shown to the left here. Occasionally, there is guidance for the right hand, too, in which case the abbreviations R.H. (right hand) and L.H. (left hand) are used to avoid confusion.

Playing styles

When it comes to hand positions, some bass players grip the neck of the bass with the palm of their hand flat against the neck of the bass and their thumb over the top of the neck. Others have their thumb positioned at the back of the neck behind the second finger of their left (or fingering) hand. The first of these playing styles looks cool, but it is the second position described that guarantees not to cause you problems with tension or stress in your hands.

The best and most comfortable left-hand position is to place your thumb approximately at the halfway point of the curve at the back of the neck opposite the second finger. Try this while playing the major, minor and pentatonic scales in Chapter 5. More information and tips about keeping comfortable hand positions while playing scales can be found on pages 54 and 56.

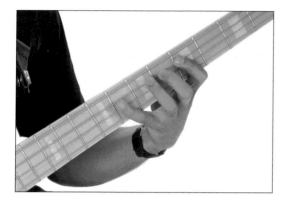

Comfortable left-hand position and fingering as seen from the front.

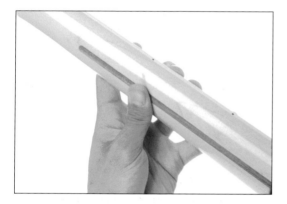

Closeup of left-hand position as seen from the back. Note the comfortable thumb position at the halfway point on the curve of the back of the neck, opposite the second finger.

Right-hand positioning for basic play. (See also the positioning for slap technique on page 40.) You will only need to use your thumb, first and second fingers to play the strings directly or use a pick at a basic level.

Fingerstyle

Most bass players will use a combination of fingers to pluck the strings of their bass guitar. It's worth learning all the techniques, then developing your own fingerstyle to suit the way you play.

Train the first and second fingers of your right hand to 'walk' on the strings until the sounds are consistent for both fingers.

Different techniques

Some bass players use only their thumb to replicate and reinforce the fat sound of a gut-strung, acoustic bass, or of a flatwound-strung bass guitar. Others use their first (index) or second (middle) finger indiscriminately, as the mood takes them, without any thought to technique.

Some of the world's best players spend many years developing techniques using a combination of thumb and first, second and third fingers – Canadian jazz player Alain Caron and Gary Willis of jazz fusion band Tribal Tech are two players who have done this to great effect.

Some bass guitarists will rake their fingers across the strings to aid in string-crossing techniques, or to copy the sounds of a jazz double bass.

Using the first and second fingers

Training the first and second fingers of your right hand (R.H.) to work alternately on the bass guitar is a good skill to develop. In this exercise (Track 2), use the right-hand fingering indicated in the notation – 1 2 1 2 1 2 1 2 – as if the fingers were walking.

One of the problems encountered with this playing style is that the first and second fingers of most people's hands are of different lengths, and they also have differing degrees of strength. Thus,

playing alternate fingers – 1 2 – on a bar of single note eighth notes will sound lopsided at first. That is, one finger will put too much emphasis on either the beat or on the 'and' of the beat. You have to practise until you achieve a string of constant eighth sounds consistent in their execution.

Practise using the first and second fingers of your right hand (R.H.) when following Track 2. Refer to Chapter 4 for help with reading the notation and tablature shown above.

Track 2

Another exercise

Another way to practise alternate plucking would be to go to page 54 and use the major scale as an exercise. Playing a major scale with alternate right-hand fingering can be surprisingly difficult. Most beginners take quite a while to achieve alternate first and second finger plucking, particularly when ascending and descending on the major scale.

Stroking the strings

Another thing to watch out for is to use as much flesh at the tips of the fingers as possible. Try not to pluck from under the strings as if you were finger-picking on a 6-string guitar, but stroke the finger across the strings to achieve that fat, bass sound.

must know

Rake The action of dragging one finger across two, or more, strings. This can be done with an open, or left hand-damped, sound. **String crossing** Moving from one string to another in a scalar passage.

Using a pick / plectrum

A lot of bass players will at some point want to use a plectrum, or pick, to play the bass guitar. For some, using the plectrum will come as second nature, while, for others, it will take a lot of consistent practice.

Plectrum technique

Here, we will demonstrate only the basics of plectrum technique, but remember that every scale, exercise and piece that you play fingerstyle can also be played with a plectrum. All of which automatically doubles up the amount of practice that you can do!

Indicated on the notation below are down and up signs above the notes. These are the same as the down and up signs for classical violin, cello or double bass music.

The plectrum should be held between the thumb and the first knuckle of the index finger.

Be systematic in your practice, and practise playing all down strokes as well as alternate down and up strokes.

It is a very good idea to alternate between using both fingerstyle and a plectrum on gigs and while practising. This will accustom the hands to the

Track 3

Practise Track 3 using a plectrum. The symbols for the right hand (R.H.) show the down and up strokes. Refer to Chapter 4 for help with reading the notation and tablature.

Hold the plectrum between your thumb and the knuckle of your index finger while you are following Track 3.

different positions. The plectrum can be used anywhere on the string. Over the end of the fingerboard produces a very fat, mellow tone. You can also play over either pickup, or near the bridge if you want a thin, abrasive tone.

Plectrum thickness

If you are wondering what thickness of pick to use on the bass guitar, the answer is to use whatever suits you. This author varies between a very sturdy, oval, white pick that gives a thick tone, and sometimes a relatively thin pick, which tends to overcome those occasional days when all technique and skill seem to have fled.

As the author and teacher, I used to think that only a thick plectrum would give the right tone, but I have learnt a lot from my students, one of whom had an amazing pick technique using a very thin plectrum on a P-Bass. I tried out his technique and, in some circumstances, it sounds absolutely amazing to use a thin pick.

must know

Many great bass players use the plectrum for a punchier sound. Carol Kaye (see page 156) was one of the earliest proponents of the plectrum on thousands of recordings. Three of Frank Zappa's bass players – Tom Fowler, Arthur Barrow and Scott Thunes – have been incredibly dextrous with it. Jazz bassist Steve Swallow achieves a very mellow sound on his custom instrument – he can be heard on many recordings with Carla Bley.

Slap technique

Slap is a high-force technique using the thumb and first finger of the right hand. Here we show you how to get the basics together. You will need to practice it a lot to sound at all good.

With your thumb pointing up, position your right hand over the E string at the bottom fret.

Rotate your whole forearm so that the thumb strikes the E string while the first finger slips under the D string ready to pluck.

Basic technique

There are two components to this technique: a thumb strike and a follow-on pluck of an octave (an eighth note) above with the first finger.

Place your right arm, which is doing the slapping, so that your thumb strikes the E string at the bottom fret. Some people point their thumbs up, others point down, but this teacher would suggest that you point your thumb up, towards yourself. The place on the thumb where you strike the string should be about halfway between the knuckle and the tip of the thumb.

The movement of the arm, when slapping, should be done from the elbow. That is, you should rotate the whole of your forearm and not just your wrist.

The follow-on plucking of the octave is achieved by the same rotation of the forearm. So, when the thumb strikes the E string, for instance, then the first finger will slip under the D string. Then, as the arm turns, your finger will naturally pluck the D string. You should not attempt to make a separate movement of the index finger or, indeed, a plucking motion with that finger. The slapping and plucking are created by the rotation of the arm.

The plucking part of this technique is often referred to as popping.

Practising slap technique

Look at the music notation, and you will see that we are working first with a stopped G, at the third fret on the E string. Make sure that you make a strong, clear sound. It should be a good thump and not a quiet tap. Then, do the same motion on the C, at the third fret on the A string.

Then move on to octave G, between the E and D strings. You can try alternating between a long, held upper octave and a short, staccato pluck. It is more usual to have the staccato sound. After that, move across to the octave between the A and G strings.

One thing to watch out for is that your strings should be relatively new, and fresh, roundwound strings. You will not be able to achieve a bright sound with dead strings.

The same exercises can also be done on the open E and A strings. It is much more difficult to control the open strings, so make sure that you damp them when playing the upper octaves.

Listen to slap bass from the likes of Larry Graham (with Sly & The Family Stone and Graham Central Station), Stanley Clarke, Marcus Miller, Bootsy Collins, Flea from the Red Hot Chili Peppers and, in the UK, Mark King.

The slapping track above is a good introduction to this great technique. Guidance for both the right hand (R.H.) and left hand (L.H.) is given. Refer to Chapter 4 for help with reading the notation and tablature.

Track 4

must know

The double bass has been slapped since the beginning of the 20th century and, possibly, even earlier. Milt Hinton and Slam Stewart were two of the finest at slapping, and also at bowing and pizzicato techniques.
Larry Graham developed slap techniques on the bass guitar.

Warm-up exercises

It's very important to build up stamina and dexterity in your fingering and plucking hands, and equally important to do so without causing RSI (repetitive strain injury). Here are two exercises that will help you to achieve this.

Track 5

Warm-up exercise 1

This exercise should be played very slowly at first to lessen the strain on the muscles of both hands. There are many variations that can be played on these patterns, but the ones shown here are among the most helpful.

The aim is to get the second and third fingers, and also the third and fourth fingers, of the left hand to work independently and as efficiently as the first two fingers. Remember to keep your fingertips right behind each fret.

Eventually, these patterns can be built up to greater speeds, but this will take months of slow and consistent practice to achieve without causing any damage to your wrists and fingers.

must know

• Take breaks away from your instrument.
• Do other activities that use larger muscle groups, such as swimming or walking.
• Pain is a warning sign – take heed of it.

Ex.2 ♩= 60

Warm-up exercise 2

Track 6

This is the author's own exercise developed to tackle the problem of persuading the second, third and fourth fingers of the playing hand to work as well as the first, second and third do together. Also, fingers 2 and 3 are on the same tendon, so it can take many hours of very slow practice to make them work with any level of independence.

Bars 1 and 2 are based on the top five notes of the B minor blues scale *(see page 64)*. This is exactly the kind of pattern that most beginning bass players will play with fingers 1, 2 and 3. While keeping the hand in exactly the same position over the G and D strings, play bars 3 and 4 with the second, third and fourth fingers. Move backwards and forwards between the two segments of scales without moving the playing hand, but using the fingering as indicated by the numbers below the notes.

Over the weeks, this will help you to build up stamina and, if done sensibly and slowly at first, should help you to avoid tendonitis. If you do find that the tendons in your wrist hurt after playing, see a doctor and arrange physiotherapy. Athletes take care of themselves, and so should musicians.

Refer to Chapter 4 if you need help with reading the notation and tablature for the warm-up exercises.

need to know more?
weblinks
• British Association for Performing Arts Medicine:
www.bapam.org.uk
• RSI Awareness:
www.rsi.org.uk
• Musicians Union:
www.musiciansunion.org.uk

4 Reading music

This section gives the basic information that you need in order to be able to read music. There are also some tips on the use of tablature. Don't worry, we will be going at a very slow pace. Learning to read conventional notation is a fantastic skill to learn, and essential for any serious musician. In the chapters that follow, you will have plenty of opportunity to practise reading skills.

Conventional notation

In conventional music notation, the stave is a grid of five lines and four spaces. On this are bars, notes and other symbols. The sooner you learn how to read notation on the stave, the sooner you can dispense with other diagrams and written aids.

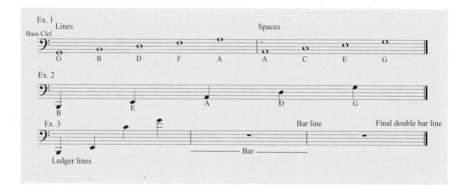

Example 1

If you look at Ex.1, above, you will see a bass clef – a stylised medieval letter F with the two dots centred on the F line. (Another common symbol here would be a treble clef, which is a G-shaped symbol centred on the G line, but we bassists use mostly the bass clef.)

The musical alphabet that we use consists of seven letters – ABCDEFG. They are positioned on the stave as shown in Ex.1, and the way to learn these positions is to use the mnemonics in the box, left.

Example 2

In Ex.2, the strings of the five-string bass guitar are indicated – from low B to high G. (The four-string bass is without the low B string.)

Example 3

Ex. 3 shows some of the other rudiments of notation. Ledger lines extend the range of the stave to include all of the notes on your instrument. A bar is shown by single bar lines at either end. A double bar line indicates the end of a piece or section.

Example 4

Ex. 4, below, shows the various types of note lengths that we will be using in this book. The American terms are on the left, and the English terms are on the right. The American terms are used for notes and rests in this book, because they are easy to memorise. Ex. 4 also shows the fractional relationship between notes: two quarter notes in a half note, etc.

Example 5

In Ex.5, bottom, are the rests that correspond to the note lengths.

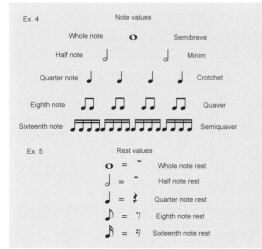

Key, time and tempo

You also need to know about signatures and the three accidental symbols in conventional notation, and how to establish the beat in a piece of music with or without the aid of a metronome.

Example 1: time signatures

A time signature is placed after the clef on the stave. The top number is number of beats in a bar. The bottom number is what kind of note. In this case, 4/4 indicates four quarter notes in each bar.

Example 2: accidentals

An accidental is a sign that either raises a note by a semitone (up one fret) - called a sharp; or a sign which lowers it by a semitone (down one fret) - called a flat. The natural sign is used either to return a note to its original pitch, or to show that it is still at its original pitch. The effect of an accidental lasts only for one bar, or measure.

Example 3: key signatures

A key signature shows which scale to play on the bass. The key signature here is made up of all sharps.

Ex. 1 Time Signature

Ex. 2 Accidentals   ♯ = Sharp   ♮ = Natural   ♭ = Flat

Ex. 3 Key Signature

Using a metronome

A metronome is a great aid to help establish tempo, or beats per minute (BPM) when practising.

There are two types of metronome available: mechanical/clockwork or electronic. The clockwork metronome, which you have to wind up, will often tend to limp – tick, TOCK, tick, TOCK – so this author would always recommend a student to buy an electronic metronome.

Some electronic metronomes can give the basic time, the downbeat on the first beat of the bar, and also subdivide the beat into eighth notes, sixteenth notes or triplets. In this respect, they can be very similar to drum machines or sequencers, and these can also be used as alternatives to metronomes.

The metronome, or drum machine, should be considered as a tool for the musician but not regarded as totally indispensable. That is, the musician, and in particular the bassist, should learn to internalise the beat as well as be able to play in time with the 'click'.

If you are playing in 4/4, you can set the metronome to click on all four beats, but any style of music will swing better if you set it to click on beats 2 and 4.

A digital Korg metronome, which can be calibrated for anything from 40 to 208 beats per minute.

Tablature

This section of the book will appear to be ever so slightly contradictory. First of all, we are going to describe how tablature, which is used in the book, actually works. Then, we are going to tell you that you should try to avoid using it altogether.

What is tablature?

Tablature is a diagram showing positions on the neck of the bass guitar where you can play notes. In this book, it is set below the notation to which it relates on a grid labelled TAB, as shown below. The four lines on the grid represent the four strings on the bass

Track 7

Notation (see previous pages)

Tablature (TAB) suggesting fret positions - see detail below

Row of numbers showing left-hand fingering (see page 34)

Close-up of tablature

o here means that the E note shown in the notation above can be played on the open E string

1 here means the F note in the notation can be played at the 1st fret on the E string

2 here means the F sharp can be played at the 2nd fret on E... and so on

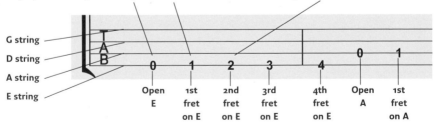

G string
D string
A string
E string

Open E · 1st fret on E · 2nd fret on E · 3rd fret on E · 4th fret on E · Open A · 1st fret on A

guitar – GDAE. The numbers refer to frets – i.e. 1 = first fret, 2 = second fret. See pages 14–15 if you are not yet familiar with frets and fret numbering. The 0 indicates an open (unfretted) string.

The tablature relates to the notation directly above it. For example, in the diagram opposite, the first note, E, is shown in four ways: as a letter; beneath which is the note itself; beneath which is an 'o' which indicates that no fingers of the left hand are to be used *(see page 34)*; beneath which is another 'o' on the bottom line of the TAB, meaning that it can be played on the open E string.

Real bassists don't use tablature

Like the fingering numbers, tablature can be a useful aid for beginners who are not yet conversant with notation. The problem is that tablature looks very definitive, and it stifles musicians from thinking for themselves. You can play an E at several places on the neck of the bass, not just at the second fret on the D string. The Internet is awash with dodgy tab sites that are set up by people who cannot, and dare not, learn how to read music properly.

Now, this author is going to suggest something quite revolutionary. Ignore the tablature in this book, or even cross it out. Remember that no professional bass player worth his or her salt would ever use tablature. Instead, use your brain. There may be one, two, or even three, places on the neck of the bass where a piece of music could be played equally well. Therefore, learn the conventional notation and how it relates to where notes can be played on the bass as quickly as you can.

Just say no. Real bassists don't use tablature.

want to know more?

• To learn how musical notes on the stave relate to playing notes on the neck of the bass guitar, follow the advice about scales and the exercise on pages 72–3.
• Ignore illegal websites that show famous tracks in the form of tablature. They infringe copyright and do not teach music properly.

weblinks
• For more information about reading bass music:
www.bassbooks.com
• For jazz-related bass books:
www.jazzwise.com
• A classic on reading for bass – Electric Bass Lines 1-6: www.carolkaye.com
• Foyles:
www.foyles.co.uk
• Chappell:
www.chappellofbond street.co.uk
• Music Sales:
www.musicsales.com

5 Finding the notes

This section covers all of the basic scales – major, minor, pentatonic and blues. It also has basic triads, which are patterns of three notes based on simple chords. We look at the modes of the major scale and the chords relating to them. These are the foundations you need to play the bass guitar in any style of music.

The major scale

Scales are musical patterns that ascend and descend an octave in tonal steps. They are foundation blocks of music, which any musician must practise. The best place to start is with a major scale, which goes up and down an octave in eight steps.

must know

There is more about the theory of scales in Chapter 7, including an explanation of intervals, which are the distances in pitch on a given scale.

Track 8

Scale in C major

Scale patterns on the bass guitar

One of the great things about the bass is that a lot of the scales work as shapes, or patterns, that can be replicated anywhere on the neck of the instrument.

You can see from the fingering shown in the notation below that this major scale starts and finishes with the second finger – 24 124 134 431 421 42. The second finger is a pivot for the rest of the fingering. Place your second finger at the third fret on the A string (as shown in the tablature below), and play the scale. You will find that you are moving only your fingers, not your hand position, on the neck.

The major scale you have just played started on note C and went up an octave to another C, then back down to C. It is called a C major scale.

You can now take the same fingering pattern, or 'shape', up and down the neck of the bass, starting with your second finger at any fret on the E or A strings.

Left-hand fingerings (see page 34) Conventional notation (see pages 46-8)

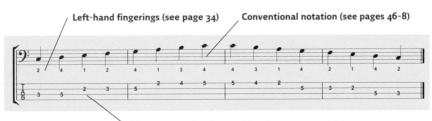

Tablature showing fret positions (see pages 50-1)

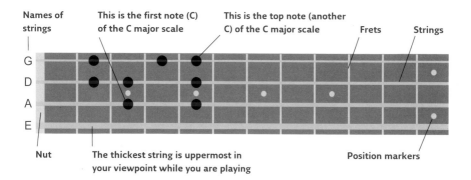

Names of strings | **This is the first note (C) of the C major scale** | **This is the top note (another C) of the C major scale** | **Frets** | **Strings**

G
D
A
E

Nut | **The thickest string is uppermost in your viewpoint while you are playing** | **Position markers**

You will find that the notes played with this pattern will always be the notes of a major scale.

Such patterns make playing the bass guitar, and reading music for the instrument, relatively simple.

Neck diagram for scale in C major

Understanding the neck diagram

In this chapter we have included diagrams of the neck of the bass guitar as an extra visual aid to show you the shape of a scale on the instrument. On the neck diagram above, the black dots show the shape of fingering positions for the C major scale in Track 8.

On the neck diagram, as on a real bass, the E string (lowest in pitch) is the thickest string, and the G string (highest in pitch) is the thinnest. However, note that the diagram looks like it's upside-down, with the order of strings reversed. This is because it reflects the way you see and relate to the neck while actually playing, not as if looking face-on.

Don't try to use the neck diagrams on their own. They do not show the order of notes or which fingers to use. That information is shown in the notation and tablature for each track *(left)*. Don't worry: once you start practising, you will soon see how the diagrams relate to each other.

> **must know**
> We haven't labelled the note names on diagrams in this chapter. Refer back to page 46 if you don't know how to identify notes on the stave. As you learn about scales, practise the exercise on pages 72-3 until you can find all the notes with ease.

must know

The other thing to remember at this point is that the thumb should always be placed about halfway around the neck, and that the thumb should always be behind the second finger (see page 35). The palm of the hand should be kept away from the back of the neck. A lot of beginners, and even some experienced players, will grip the neck of the bass with the thumb over the top of the neck.

One of the temptations with having recordings, as well as fingering, tablature and neck diagrams, is that you will quickly learn to play pieces of music from memory and not need to read the notation at all. This is not a bad thing in itself. As long as you are learning the patterns involved in the notation, then you are learning to understand and play – all music is made up of these patterns. However, most readers will benefit greatly from learning how to read music. To do this takes time, practice, patience and persistence. For reading exercises, see Chapter 8.

A tune based on the major scale

Following on from the major scale practice on the previous pages, this a short piece based on the same scale. Listen to the recorded track, and then play along with it while reading the notation as far as you can understand it.

The important point to remember is to keep your second finger on the root (first) note of this scale. Keep the fingers comfortably spread and, using a finger-per-fret (see page 116), you will be able to play all of the notes 'under the hand'. That is, you will not need to move your hand position and, especially, you will not need to look at your hand.

Remember that, if the notes of the tune go up in steps, play them using the same fingering that you would for the scale.

Track 9

A tune based on the major scale

The minor scale

As with the major scale, the minor scale encompasses eight steps up and down an octave, and the fingering can be used as a movable pattern anywhere on the neck of the bass guitar.

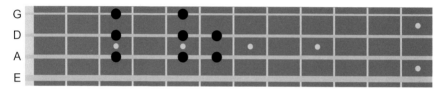

Neck diagram for scale in C minor

The minor scale is also called the natural minor scale or the Aeolian mode (see page 74 for more on modes).

Like the major scale on the previous pages, the minor scale shown here starts and ends on C on the third fret of the A string. This time, however, you start with the first finger instead of the second. The full fingering is shown in the notation below – 134 134 13 31 431 431. The set of notes is slightly different from those of the C major scale on the previous pages. It is a C minor scale.

Compare the sound of the C major and C minor scales, and their notation, and you will immediately hear and see the difference in character, even though some of the notes, or pitches, are the same. The distances between pitches on a scale are called

> **must know**
> The minor scale has different intervals to the major scale and is said to sound 'sad'. For more on theory, see pages 104–9.

Track 10

Scale in C minor

intervals, and they are an important concept to grasp about scales. For more on intervals, see pages 107–9.

The minor scale pattern shown can be placed at any point starting on the E or A strings, and it will always look and sound like a minor scale.

When playing the minor scale, remember to keep your thumb behind the second finger. This will help your hand to stay in a comfortable position, and also give an even spread to the hand when you are playing with a finger-per-fret. For more about playing with a finger-per-fret, see page 116.

There is another fingering for the minor scale, which works across four strings. Place your fourth finger on the C at the eighth fret of the E string, and use the fingering 4 124 124 1.

A tune based on the minor scale

There are several different ways that you can play the tune below, which is based on the notes of the minor scale. You could easily play it from the open A string, for example. However, the fingering and tablature show how to play it using the fourth finger on A as a starting note.

You could also use the fingering shown in the main diagram on the previous page, and play some of the piece starting on your first finger. Then you would need to move your hand position for the last part. Try it out using these variations.

must know

Major and minor scales look like they have eight notes each. However, because the eighth note sounds like it repeats the first note (only up an octave), the scales are said to have only **seven** distinct notes. Likewise, pentatonic scales are considered to have only **five** distinct notes ('pent' = five), because the sixth note repeats the first on the octave. See chapter 7 for more music theory.

Track 11

A tune based on the minor scale

Major pentatonic scale

In contrast with the scales on the previous pages, pentatonic scales have only five distinct notes *(see must know box opposite)*. Think of the major pentatonic scale as the same as the major scale on page 54, but without the fourth and seventh notes.

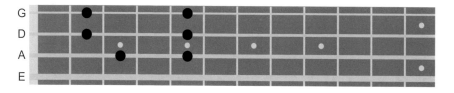

Neck diagram for a
C major pentatonic scale

In music theory, the fourth and seventh notes of the major scale are said to cause 'tension' because they can sometimes sound discordant when played alongside other notes. The major pentatonic scale omits these notes and so avoids potential clashes.

You could play C major pentatonic notes on your bass guitar without clashing, say, with a piano playing C major chords (chords are sets of notes usually played together). Playing a tune over chords in this way is called improvising.

The major pentatonic scale is used in a wide variety of folk music traditions, from Indonesian gamelan to American blues music. Jazz saxophonists of the 1930s made great use of it, too.

Track 12

C major pentatonic scale

Minor pentatonic scale

You can think of the minor pentatonic scale as the same as the natural minor scale on page 57, but without that scale's second or flat sixth notes. The minor pentatonic is a very cool scale, and is used to great effect in a lot of rock, blues and fusion music.

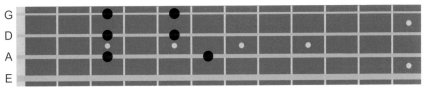

**Neck diagram for a
C minor pentatonic scale**

As you can see from the neck diagram above, the minor pentatonic scale has a simple shape. It starts at the first note of the C minor scale.

You can play the C minor pentatonic on your bass guitar while someone else plays a C minor chord on another instrument, such as a guitar. You can make a typical rock sound with this, particularly when playing riffs (repeated patterns).

If you want to be more experimental, try the scale starting from G minor while someone else plays a C minor chord on another instrument. From this you will see that the simple pentatonic shape can be used to create quite complex musical phrases.

Track 13

C minor pentatonic scale

Inversions of pentatonic scales

'Inversions' are ways of playing sets of notes from a parent scale. They are really good fingering practice for the left hand on the fingerboard. The examples here are based on the minor pentatonic scale from the previous page.

The first bar of Track 14 is the ascending part of the minor pentatonic scale on the previous page, called here the root position, or parent scale. The next bar, labelled 1st inversion, starts with the second note of that scale. The 2nd inversion starts with the third, and so on. You will soon grasp the concept when you start playing along, but take care with the fingerings, which differ from one inversion to the next.

A fascinating thing about pentatonic scales is that when a minor pentatonic scale is taken as the root (C minor in this example), the first inversion will be a major pentatonic scale (Eᵇ major here).

Advanced readers who have mastered the minor pentatonic scale in all positions could try practising it in all 12 keys. (See the cycle of fifths on page 106 for help with this.) Then some really fun stuff: try using the minor pentatonic scale and all the inversions to write your own riffs.

Four inversions of a minor pentatonic scale (see the next page for their neck diagrams)

Track 14

> **must know**
> Listen out for inversions of minor pentatonic scales in Stevie Wonder's Sir Duke (1977) and Master Blaster (1980), and Frank Zappa's King Kong (1968).

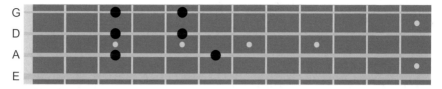

Neck diagram for the root position of Track 14 on previous page

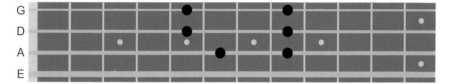

Inversion 1

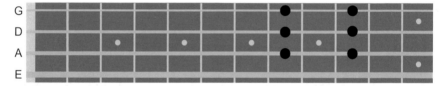

Inversion 2

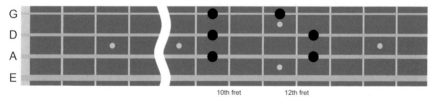

10th fret   12th fret

Inversion 3 (higher up the fingerboard)

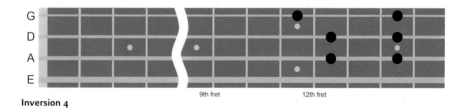

9th fret   12th fret

Inversion 4

A tune based on pentatonic scales

The tune below is based on the major pentatonic scale, in the style of Motown or soul music *(see pages 96-7)*. You will find that you can play the whole of this tune while leaving your second finger over the root note of the major pentatonic scale.

A tune inspired by the major pentatonic

More pentatonic inspiration

George Gershwin used the major pentatonic scale as the basis of many of his compositions. For instance, most of the melody of his famous *I Got Rhythm*, published in 1930, is based on this scale.

The melody for Ray Charles' *I Got A Woman* (1954) is based on the minor pentatonic scale. In more recent times, Kanye West has sampled *I Got A Woman* for his song *Gold Digger* (2005).

Many rock tunes from the early 1970s use riffs based on the minor pentatonic scale. A good example is *Black Night* on Deep Purple's album *Deep Purple In Rock*, released in 1970. Also from 1970 is *Paranoid* from Black Sabbath's recording of the same name. See if you can identify what pentatonic scales are used in *I Shot The Sheriff* (1973) by Bob Marley, *Lady Marmalade* (1974) by Labelle, and *Billie Jean* (1983) by Michael Jackson.

When you feel confident about identifying and playing major and minor pentatonic scales, have a go at composing your own melodies based on them.

must know

The major pentatonic scale can sound simple or complex depending on the chord over which it is played. So, if you play a C major pentatonic scale over a C major chord, you are playing mostly the same tones. Whereas, if you play the same C major pentatonic over an F major chord, you have a more complex, jazzier sound.

The blues scale

The blues scale uses the so-called 'blue notes', which are a semitone lower than notes on the major scale. Blues music is based on this scale, while bass guitarists often use it to construct hard rock or heavy metal riffs.

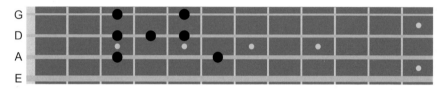

Neck diagram for a blues scale in C minor

The blues scale is most simply described as a minor pentatonic scale with a sharp fourth, or flat fifth, interval added to it. In the C minor blues scale, as shown here, the intervals consist of root, flat third, fourth, sharp fourth, fifth, flat seventh, octave (C, E♭, F, F♯, G, B♭, C). Don't worry if you don't really understand this yet; it will make more sense when you've done more lessons and become familiar with step intervals in music theory and notation.

A very good example of a classic rock tune based on the blues scale is *Heartbreaker* from the *Led Zeppelin II* album (1969).

The riff for the opening track on Black Sabbath's first album (called *Black Sabbath*, 1970) uses the blues scale. Consisting solely of the root, octave and flat fifth in the key of G minor, it makes a very dark

Track 16

Blues scale in C minor

sound. Jimi Hendrix also used this sound at the beginning of *Purple Haze* (1967), with a combination of B♭ and E in the key of E minor.

One of the classic rock riffs, Deep Purple's *Smoke On The Water* (1972), has the guitar and organ playing the first four notes of a G minor blues scale in perfect fourths. *(See page 106* for the cycle of fourths.)

Many of the more modern heavy rock bands use the flat second of the scale. This sounds similar to a musical mode called Phrygian *(see page 74)*. Bands such as Tool and The Mars Volta – who are better described as modern progressive bands rather than simply heavy – tend to use whatever scale is appropriate to the song.

A tune based on the blues scale

The tune in Track 17 is a riff in the style of a heavy metal piece of music. It is shown starting at C here, but you could transpose the riff to any key. That is, you can play it anywhere on the neck of the bass guitar. However, make sure that your hand stays in one position while playing this piece of music.

After you've practised this, why not try composing your own riffs around the blues scale?

must know
The added blue note on the blues scale is said to add 'tension', which creates the familiar bluesy sound. When we play a minor third interval over a parent major, or dominant seventh, chord in the blues, it causes a clash that sounds like the slightly flat third in some West African scales. It is often called the 'Jimi Hendrix' chord.

Track 17

A tune based on the blues scale

Triads

Triads are three-note shapes. In each, the first note is called the root, and the second and third notes are at given intervals above the root. The triads shown on these pages are the basis of many basslines, played usually as single notes rather than chords.

Major, minor, diminished and augmented triads starting on C

Track 18

There are four kinds of triads on Track 18, shown in the notation above, and in the neck diagrams over the next few pages. The four forms are called major, minor, diminished and augmented. For the sake of simplicity at this stage, the examples are rooted on the same note – C – which can be played at the third fret on the A string. We will look at each in turn.

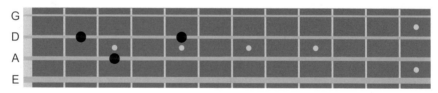

Neck diagram for a major triad starting on C

Major triads

Major triads use three notes from the major scale at intervals (distances in pitch) called root, major third and perfect fifth. (See pages 107–9 for more about intervals). You would usually play this triad with the second finger on the root note, and the other fingers placed as shown.

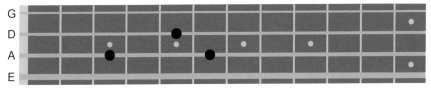

Neck diagram for a
minor triad starting on C

Minor triads

Minor triads use three notes from the minor scale at
intervals called root, minor third and perfect fifth.
You would usually play a minor triad with the first
finger on the root note, as shown in the diagrams.
However, it can also be played from the fourth finger
across three strings, starting, in the case of C minor,
from the fourth finger at the eighth fret on the E string.

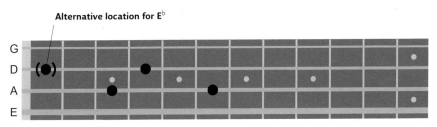

Alternative location for E♭

Diminished triads

Neck diagram for a
diminished triad starting on C,
with alternative fingerings

Diminished triads are similar to minor triads, but
instead of a perfect fifth they have a flattened fifth,
described as 'diminished'.

We bassists would usually play this with the first
finger on the root, as indicated in the notation and
tablature opposite. You could also use your third
finger on the root, with your first finger playing
E♭ on the first fret of the D string, as shown in the
neck diagram above.

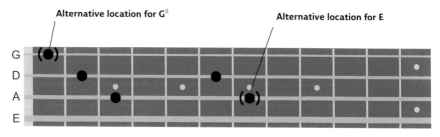

Alternative location for G♯   Alternative location for E

Neck diagram for an
augmented triad starting on C

Augmented triads

Augmented triads are similar to major triads, but the fifth is sharpened and so described as 'augmented'.

The tablature on page 66 shows how to play this with your second finger on the root note, C.

Alternatively, you can use your third finger on the root note, C, if playing the third note, G♯, at the first fret on the G string. And another alternative is to use your first finger on the root note, C, with the second note, E, at the 7th fret on the A string.

A tune based on triads

Track 19 contains major, minor and diminished triads. It is possible to play it all without moving your hand position if you follow the fingering given.

Track 19

A tune to help you understand major, minor and diminished triads

If you are a novice following this book sequentially, then you may not yet know how to identify all the information in the notation for this tune. However, you can grasp that there are different types of triads

going on in each bar. We will name the triad types in the notation to help you understand:

Bar 1 – C major and F major

Bar 2 – C major and D minor

Bar 3 – G major and C major

Bar 4 – C major and D minor (each played as second inversions from the fifth)

Bar 5 – B diminished and C major

Triads on the major scale

On the following page is another scale called the harmonised major scale. This consists of a series of triads based on the notes of the major scale (see page 54).

In Track 20, the triads are played one after the other as individual notes – the way in which bass players are most likely to play them. On other instruments, such as the guitar, the notes are often played together, which is why they are usually referred to as chords.

In the notation on page 70, you will see Roman numerals – I, II, III, IV, V, VI, VII – used to label the triads. This is a conventional way of labelling the seven steps, or degrees, of the scale and their corresponding triad chords. (Arabic numerals – 1, 2, 3 – are used for all other numbers in music notation.)

The triads at degrees I, IV and V of a major scale are always major triads; those at II, III, and VI are always minor triads. The triad at degree VII of a major scale is always diminished. (The augmented triad does not occur in the harmonised major scale.)

must know

must know

The augmented triad can often be heard at the beginning of blues, doo-wop and R'n'B tunes. Listen to the Allman Brothers' live version of Stormy Monday (1971), or the Beatles' Oh! Darling from Abbey Road (1969). The bassline in Ob-La-Di, Ob-La-Da from The Beatles' White Album (1968) is based mostly on major triads. Abracadabra (1982) by the Steve Miller Band is based on A minor, D minor and E major triads.

A series of triads based on the harmonised major scale

Track 20

Beginners should follow Track 20 using the fingering, tablature and neck diagrams shown here.

More advanced players can see how it sounds and feels starting from C on the eighth fret of the E string.

must know

The steps, or degrees, of the harmonised major scale have generic names in music theory:

I – tonic
II – supertonic
III – mediant
IV – subdominant
V – dominant
VI – submediant
VII – leading note
See Chapter 7 for more theory.

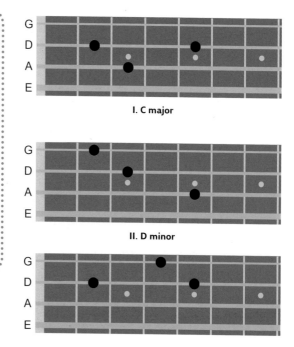

I. C major

II. D minor

III. E minor

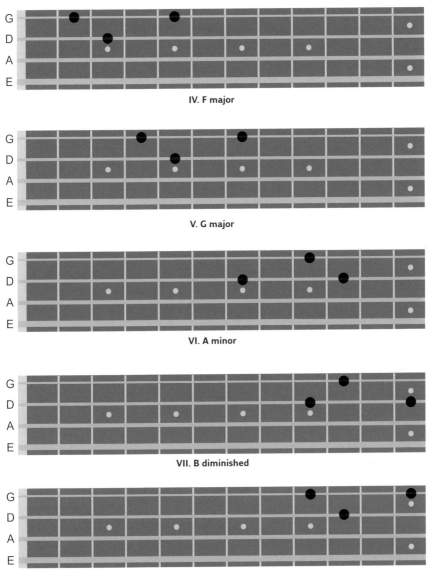

IV. F major

V. G major

VI. A minor

VII. B diminished

I. C major

How to learn notes on the neck

You can use a series of major scales to learn the location of notes on the neck of your bass guitar. This might seem like a long and boring exercise, but naming the notes out loud will help you memorise their placements.

Essential knowledge

Do this exercise each day consistently and, within a month, you will be confident about finding a note anywhere on the neck of the bass. It might feel like a slog doing it every day, but once you have thoroughly learnt your notes, you need never do this exercise again.

Note that the exercise is meant to be slow. On a metronome, the setting is 'quarter note equals 60', or 60 beats per minute. Don't try to speed up the metronome.

Memorising the notes

If you look at the top stave on the notation, you will see the same major scale as on page 54, starting and finishing on C with the second finger on the third fret of the A string. If you've been practising the scales so far, you may already be able to play this from memory, even if you don't know the names of the notes. This time you will be playing it while saying the names of the notes out loud, as labelled.

Then move your hand up one fret for another major scale, starting and ending on D♭ with your second finger on the fourth fret of the A string. Keep reciting the note names, including the flats ♭. Repeat the process for the next scale, which starts and ends

on D with your second finger on the fifth fret of the A
string. This includes sharp # notes. Then move up to E♭
with your second finger on the sixth fret of the A string.

The scales on Track 21 don't cover the whole neck,
but the same system applies to the whole neck.
After you've done the scales shown here, repeat the
process starting with a G major scale using your
second finger at the third fret on the E string.

As you move chromatically up to the top of the
fingerboard you should find that you are always
reciting seven, consecutive letter names, and never
mixing sharps and flats in the same scale.

When you've got the hang of the exercise, don't
look at the fingerboard: do it all by touch.

Track 21

**Using major scales to learn
the notes on the neck**

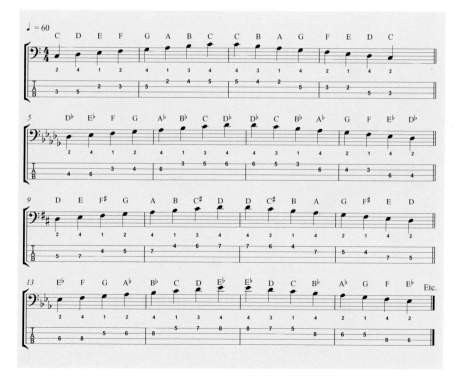

The modes

Modes are musical variations based on the seven steps of the major scale. Each mode has its own characteristics and associations in various types of music. The simplest way to describe them is to relate them to the scales you've met already.

I Ionian Based on the first degree of the major scale (C to C in C major). It is identical to the major scale on page 54. You will hear this scale in a huge variety of music, including pop, folk and classical.

II Dorian Based on the second degree of the major scale (D to D in C major). It can be thought of as a minor scale with a major sixth degree. The Dorian mode is often used in jazz, and many old English folk tunes are based on this mode.

III Phrygian 'Fridge-ian' Based on the third degree of the major scale (E to E in C major). It can be thought of as a minor scale with a flattened second degree. Typical in Spanish flamenco music.

IV Lydian Based on the fourth degree of the major scale (F to F in C major). Lydian mode can be thought of as a major scale with a raised fourth degree. It is frequently used in jazz for improvisation, particularly to spice up a major chord.

V Mixolydian Based on the fifth degree of the major scale (G to G in C major). This one can be thought of as a major scale with a flattened seventh degree. The mode can be used in the blues, and is also found in many English folk songs, particularly from the time of the Napoleonic wars (early 19th century).

VI Aeolian Based on the sixth degree of the major scale (A to A in C major).

Aeolian mode is identical to the natural minor scale on page 57, although in Track 22 it is played at a higher level. It is frequently used in rock music.

VII Locrian Based on the seventh degree of the major scale (B to B in C major). Can be thought of as a minor scale with a flattened second and a flattened fifth degree. Often used in jazz for improvisation, usually over a 'half-diminished' chord (a minor seventh, flat fifth chord).

Track 22

The modes

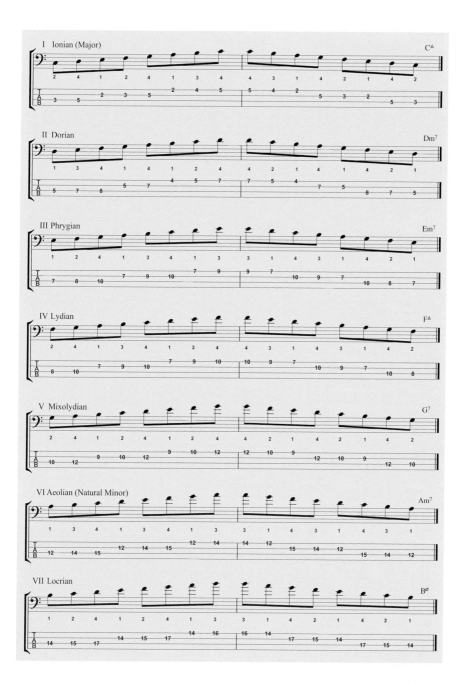

Harmonic and melodic minor

You met the natural minor scale – also known as the Aeolian mode – on pages 57 and 74–75. Now you'll meet two more scales that are based on it: the harmonic minor and melodic minor.

Harmonic C minor scale

Track 23

Harmonic minor scale

The harmonic minor scale is the simpler of the two scales because it has only one form. Compare it with the natural minor scale on page 57, and you will see that it is the same apart from that the seventh note – also called the seventh degree – is raised, as denoted by the natural symbol (see Accidentals, page 50). This means that you will play B instead of Bᵇ here.

Use the fingering as shown, and you will find that the harmonic minor scale fits neatly under the hand.

The harmonic minor scale is used in Eastern Meditteranean music, such as in the Jewish tune *Hava Nagila*, and in some Arabic music.

Neck diagram for harmonic C minor scale

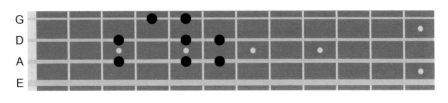

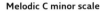

Melodic C minor scale

Melodic minor scale

In classical music, the melodic minor scale is used in ascending and descending forms. The ascending version is the natural minor scale with a major sixth and a major seventh. (In the notation above, the natural signs on the sixth and seventh notes cancel out the flats that would otherwise apply in this key.) The two notes in descending form revert to flats.

The scale was used in this way to make melodies move more smoothly. Listen to Bach's *Bourrée in E minor*, which was also used by Jethro Tull on *Stand Up*, for an example of the melodic minor scale.

In jazz, the ascending form of the melodic minor scale is used in its own right for improvisation.

Track 24

Neck diagrams for the melodic C minor scale

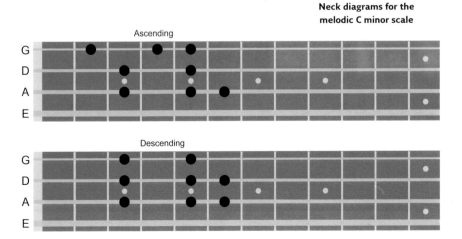

Four-note arpeggios

Arpeggios are chords – groups of notes – that are played quite rapidly in succession, rather than sounded together. They are used a lot in modern rock improvisation because they are a relatively simple way to add melodic colour to a piece.

Four-note arpeggios

Track 25

The arpeggios of four-note chords shown on these pages are based on the basic triads on the harmonised major scale that you encountered on pages 70–1. The ascending patterns can be played either across three strings, as shown, or across all four strings starting at the eighth fret on the E string. You can also play them as descending patterns. Their symbols are included in the captions here.

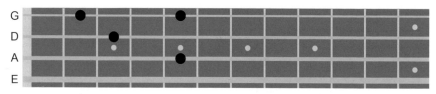

C△ = C major triad with a major seventh on the top (C major 7)

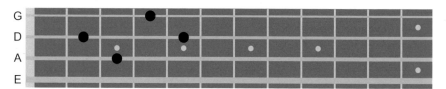

Dm7 = D minor triad with a minor seventh on the top (D minor 7)

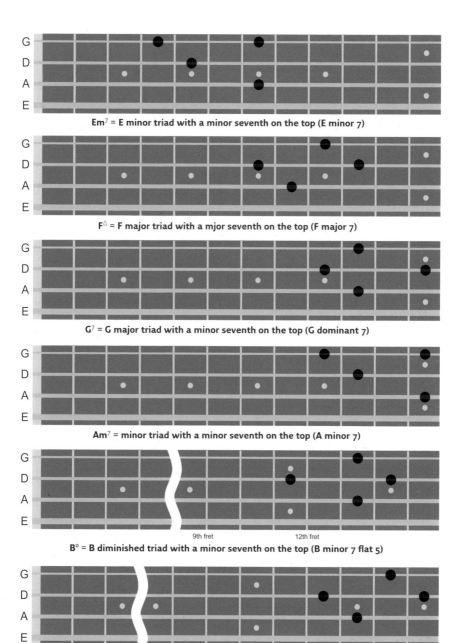

Em⁷ = E minor triad with a minor seventh on the top (E minor 7)

F△ = F major triad with a mjor seventh on the top (F major 7)

G⁷ = G major triad with a minor seventh on the top (G dominant 7)

Am⁷ = minor triad with a minor seventh on the top (A minor 7)

Bᵉ = B diminished triad with a minor seventh on the top (B minor 7 flat 5)

C△ = C major triad with a major seventh on the top (C major 7)

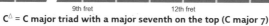

Two-octave scales

When you feel comfortable with the one-octave major and minor scales at the beginning of this chapter, you can progress to scales that span two octaves.

Two-octave major scale

Track 26

Track 27

Two-octave minor scale

Arrows show that you are moving your finger over two frets

The fingering shown in both of these examples give a smooth and consistent way to ascend and descend the neck of the instrument. Practise them both slowly at first (at 60 beats per minute), and then build up the tempo over the coming weeks.

Grooves and riffs

These examples show some typical bass grooves on one pitch. Rhythms like these are often played together with a drummer's patterns on bass drum.

Ex. 1 is a typical rhythm used in rock, Latin and other styles. It is derived from Brazilian *baion* rhythm. The count is 1 (and 2) and 3 (and 4 and) – nothing is played on the bracketed parts of the count.

Ex. 2 is a rhythm often used in funk or jazz-fusion music. The count is taken from the sixteenth-note subdivision *(see page 47 for divisions)*. The dotted eighth note plus sixteenth-note subdivision of the first beat sounds like the rhythm of the word 'Charleston' *(see also pages 135–6)*.

Ex. 3 is typical funk rhythm. In this one you are playing the first two sixteenth notes of the first beat, and the last two sixteenth notes of the second beat. The recording demonstrates exactly how to play it.

Ex. 4 is a variation on the first rhythm, but instead of playing the second note on the 'and' of two, you play it on the last sixteenth note of two. Keep the sixteenth-note subdivision firmly in place. Listen to the sound, and you will soon get the idea.

More tips on how to read and play sixteenth-note rhythms can be found in Chapter 9.

Grooves on one pitch

Track 28

want to know more?

• This chapter covers the basic scales, but there are many more scales and variations that you can learn
• Jimmy Haslip's The Melodic Bass Library (Warner, 1995) is a good sourcebook

weblinks
• www.bassbooks.com
• www.jazzwise.com

6 Bass styles

In this chapter we will be looking at common styles and rhythms used in popular music: rock 'n' roll and doo-wop, country, reggae, samba, bossa nova and salsa, Motown and Stax-type basslines, and the basics of how to create a walking bassline in jazz. By the end of this chapter, you will have a greater understanding of these styles and how to play the different basslines for them.

Rock 'n' roll and doo-wop

Rock 'n' roll emerged in 1950s America and became a worldwide phenomenon, spawning other genres that are now collectively called rock music. Doo-wop was also popular in the 50s and still provides inspiring basslines for musicians today.

must know

Arguably, Jackie Brenston's Rocket 88 (1951) was the first true rock 'n' roll recording. The band playing on this track was Ike Turner's Kings of Rhythm, for whom Brenston also played tenor saxophone. However, the band was later mistakenly credited as Jackie Brenston and His Delta Cats.

Rock 'n' roll

Rock 'n' roll evolved from a cross-fertilisation of Afro-American boogie and swing music, and the white American styles of hillbilly and country swing.

In the Afro-American community, artists such as Arthur "Big Boy" Crudup (*That's All Right*, 1947), Big Mama Thornton (Leiber and Stoller's *Hound Dog*, 1952), and Wynonie Harris (*Good Rockin' Tonight*, 1947) are credited as the forerunners of rock 'n' roll.

The country roots of rock 'n' roll can clearly be heard in the songs of artists such as Hank Williams (*Move It On Over*, 1947), Chet Atkins (*The Nashville Jump*, 1947) and Merle Travis (*Louisiana Boogie*, 1952).

The genre of rock 'n' roll was well established by the mid-50s, as exemplified by songs such as Bill Haley's *Rock Around The Clock* (1954), and Elvis Presley's version of Arthur Crudup's *That's All Right* (1954).

Other famous rock 'n' roll artists include Carl Perkins, Fats Domino, Little Richard, Jerry Lee Lewis and Chuck Berry. The typical rock 'n' roll band would have one or two guitars, a bass or (after the mid-1950s) an electric bass guitar, and drums.

The term 'rockabilly' is a sub-genre of rock 'n' roll that incorporated country influences and has been applied to many white musicians, including Presley, Perkins, Lewis and Hayley.

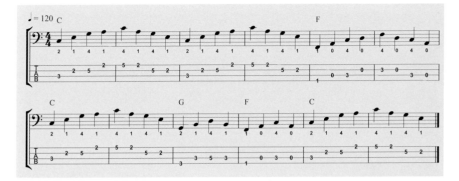

12-bar blues

The music example on Track 29 is a typical rock 'n' roll bassline. It uses a very common chord progression, or sequence, called 12-bar blues.

To analyse the composition of 12-bar blues, look closely at the notation above. You will see that we have written the first note of each chord above the stave. The chords that span two or four bars contain five notes each at intervals of root, third, fifth, sixth and octave. The chords that span a single bar contain only three notes at intervals of root, third and fifth. There are 12 bars altogether. Countless songs in popular music use sequences like this.

Doo-wop

The Afro-American vocal style of doo-wop originated in the 1930s and 40s. Two notable close-harmony male vocal groups at that time were the Mills Brothers and the Ink Spots. In common with the all-girl Andrews Sisters, they combined precision harmonies with swing arrangements.

Rock 'n' roll, 12-bar blues bassline

Track 29

must know

The rock 'n' roll 12-bar blues sample here is a type of 'walking bassline', similar to those found in jazz. For more on jazz walking basslines, see pages 100-1.

A rumba-style doo-wop bassline

Track 30

Doo-wop broke into the mainstream in the 1950s. Some of the best exponents were The Orioles (*Baby, Please Don't Go*, 1951, and *Crying In The Chapel*, 1953), The Ravens (*Rock Me All Night Long*, 1952) and The 5 Royales (*Dedicated To The One I Love*, 1957).

In the 70s and 80s, Frank Zappa recorded several versions of some of his favourite 50s doo-wop songs, including *The Closer You Are* (Earl Lewis and the Channels) and *Valarie* (Jackie and the Starlites).

Sample doo-wop bassline

Track 30 is a piece written by the author with a rumba-style doo-wop bassline in the key of C major.

If you look at the notation for this piece, you will see a sequence of triad chords, which are labelled with the Roman numerals I, VI, IV, V according to which degree of the harmonised major scale they use *(see pages 69–71)*.

If you want to understand more about the rhythm of this piece, go through the lessons about rhythm in Chapter 8. You will then be able to see that this piece subdivides the bar of eighth notes into 123 123 12.

Country

Country music encompasses a large range of styles in the USA, including bluegrass, western swing, honky tonk, cowboy music and the Nashville sound. Here we look at just a few notable artists who might provide inspiration for your bass playing.

The Carter Family

Among the early pioneers of country music was The Carter Family band, which recorded from 1927 to 1943. The three original family members were from Virginia, and their music was influenced by the harmonies of mountain gospel music. Maybelle Carter developed an original technique on the guitar known as 'frailing', which involves playing on the bass strings with a thumb pick while keeping the rhythm and harmony going with other fingers. A good example of their style is *Will The Circle Be Unbroken* (1928).

Jimmie Rodgers

Jimmie Rodgers is often called the father of country music. He began life working on the railroads, which gave rise to his nickname, the singing brakeman. Though stricken with tuberculosis at the age of 27, he became a major recording star from that time until his death in 1933, at the age of 35. *Blue Yodel No. 1* and *TB Blues* are great recordings.

Bob Wills

In a period from 1935 to 1945, Bob Wills and his Texas Playboys created a fusion of big-band swing and country, known as western swing. If you have

must know

Most country basslines are relatively simple, consisting of the root and fifth of each chord with some passing tones. The music of artists such as Bill Monroe, Bob Wills and Johnny Cash can be accompanied by a 'two-feel' on the bass guitar or double bass (see page 89). The edges between swing, country and rock 'n' roll are blurred, especially in the western swing of Bob Wills.

never listened to Bob Wills before, check out *Steel Guitar Rag* (1933). His *New San Antonio Rose* is another classic, recorded as an instrumental tune in 1938, and in a vocal version in 1944. You might notice similarities with the music of Woody Herman, Glenn Miller and Tommy Dorsey.

Bill Monroe

The American roots music known as bluegrass was closely associated with Bill Monroe and his band, the Blue Grass Boys, from 1936 until Monroe's death in 1996. Bluegrass is an up-tempo, Kentucky version of Scottish and Irish jigs and reels. Musicians such as Monroe combined these styles with elements of the blues to create a musical art form that still delights audiences today.

Typically, a bluegrass band uses stringed instruments such as the resonator guitar (an acoustic guitar with metal resonators), fiddle, banjo, double bass and mandolin. Earl Scruggs and Lester Flatt were both members of Bill Monroe's Blue Grass Boys; they later formed their own band, the Foggy Mountain Boys. Listen to a compilation such as *Bluegrass Bonanza* to get an idea of the sound.

Track 31

A country bassline

Johnny Cash

The long career of Johnny Cash began in 1955 at Sun Records alongside the likes of Elvis Presley, Carl Perkins, Jerry Lee Lewis and Roy Orbison. Two of Johnny Cash's greatest recordings were made when he went to entertain the prisoners at Folsom and San Quentin prisons in 1968-9. His second wife, country singer June Carter *(see page 87)* collaborated on some records. Towards the end of Cash's life, he made several outstanding albums with the producer Rick Rubin *(American Recordings I-V)*, in particular *IV: The Man Comes Around*. He died in 2003, aged 71.

Other artists

A generation of 'country rock' musicians made recordings in the 1960s and 70s. Most prominent among these were The Byrds (*Sweetheart Of The Rodeo*, 1968), The Flying Burrito Brothers (*The Gilded Palace Of Sin*, 1969), Gram Parsons (*GP*, 1973, and *Grievous Angel*, 1974, both of which feature duets with Emmylou Harris), Michael Nesmith (*Magnetic South*, 1970) and The Nitty Gritty Dirt Band, who collaborated with bluegrass and country players in their fine album *Will The Circle Be Unbroken* (1972).

A sample bassline for country

The example bassline in Track 31 would make an excellent introduction to a Johnny Cash-style country tune in the Folsom Prison period of his career. It is based around chords I, IV and V (in this case C, F and G) in the key of C. It has a 'two-feel' to it, which is when a piece of music is counted in four, but the bass and drums play 'in two' with the half note, rather than the quarter note, as the pulse.

must know

Highly recommended recordings:
- Johnny Cash At Folsom Prison (Columbia, 1968)
- Johnny Cash At San Quentin (Columbia, 1969)
- Bluegrass Bonanza (Properbox, 2006)
- Bill Monroe: Gotta Travel On (MCA, 2003)
- Jimmie Rodgers: The Singing Brakeman (Sanctuary, 2006)
- Bob Wills: The King Of Western Swing (ASV, 1998)

Reggae

Jamaica is home to many music styles, including African drum rhythms, music of the Pocomania church, fife and drum quadrilles, and jonkanoo festival music. A cross-fertilisation between the older styles has created mento, ska and, most famously, reggae.

must know

Mento basslines can be similar to Cuban rhythms, but often they are simple 'two-feel' bass patterns – the emphasis is on the half note, instead of quarter note. Ska is a faster style, like a shuffle but with the emphasis on the 'and' of the beat. Usually the bassline for ska will be a relatively simple 'walking' line of quarter notes. Reggae is, in general, slower than ska with more complex basslines.

Mento

In the 1950s, businessman Stanley Motta set up a recording studio in Kingston to record some local folk music, called mento. This rural style of music is often compared with Trinidadian calypso. However, mento tends to contain more lyrical innuendo than calypso, and virtuosic improvised banjo lines. The bass instrument is the rhumba box, which has keys on a resonator box. Good examples of mento are Lord Messam's version of *Linstead Market*, Baba Motta and His Jamaicans' *She Pon Top* and The Jamaican Calypsonians' *Dr. Kinsey*. Spot the innuendo in the rhyming of 'Kinsey Report' with 'favourite indoor sport'.

Jamaican dancehalls and ska

After the Second World War, those Jamaicans in Kingston who could afford radios would listen to the American R 'n' B coming across from stations in Miami, New Orleans and Nashville. It was also at this time that powerful sound systems started to be used in the dancehalls of Kingston. Headley Jones, an RAF radio engineer, and another engineer, Mr Morrison, constructed enormous amplifiers that split the treble and bass frequencies to different sized speakers – 18in., 15in. and tweeters.

Among the first dancehall DJs were Count Machuki at the 'Tom the Great Sebastian' sound system – an early rapper in the 1950s. After him came Clement 'Coxsone' Dodd, Duke Reid and Vincent 'King' Edwards. All these DJs recorded fresh ska music to play on their sound systems, too.

Jamaican musicians who played at the uptown hotels for high society also came downtown to record for dancehalls. Listen to The Duke Reid Group's *Rude Boy*, The Skatalites' *Don De Lion* and Roland Alphonso's *James Bond* to get a feel for this style of music. Much of the ska from the 1950s and 60s is a Jamaican take on the American jump and shuffle style of R 'n' B, which was being imported and played on the radio at the time.

Rastafarian influence

The Rastafarian community lived outside mainstream Jamaican society from the 1930s onwards, inspired by the philosophy of the Jamaican nationalist hero Marcus Garvey (1887–1940), and accepting the Emperor Haile Selassie I of Ethiopia (1892–1975) as the symbol of God incarnate, or Jah. A culture of black separatism and concentration on all things Afrocentric, plus the use of marijuana as a spiritual aid, became features of the Rastafari movement in Jamaica.

In 1960, Count Ossie – a Rastafarian who practised the movement's religious *nyabinghi* drumming – was persuaded by Kingston musician Prince Buster to play on the song *Oh Carolina*. Released as a single, this was the first example of Rastafarian drumming on a deeply un-spiritual ska dancehall song, and it is considered by many as the first reggae recording.

A reggae bassline

Track 32

The best-known reggae artist is, of course, Bob Marley (1945–81). His early recordings in the 1960s are particularly interesting: *Nice Time*, *Trenchtown Rock* and the early version of *Stir It Up*, which are all available on compilation albums.

The first Fender® bass guitar and amplifier were brought to Jamaica by Byron Lee in about 1959; until then the double bass had been the instrument used by such players as Lloyd Brevett with the Skatalites.

There are two basic types of reggae drum rhythm: the 'four drop' with the bass drum playing on all four beats, and the 'one drop' with the bass drum playing just on the second half of the bar.

Example of a reggae bass pattern

The musical example in Track 32 would arguably work very well as the introduction for a Bob Marley-style reggae tune. It is similar to the lines played by Jamaican bass player Aston 'Family Man' Barrett, who is said to be responsible for many of the basslines on Bob Marley's recordings.

Reggae bass patterns can often be improvised under a vocal line. This short piece reflects the kind of movement that might be done, particularly with the flat seventh in bar 3.

Samba, bossa nova and salsa

The music of Brazil and Cuba is drawn from a diverse palette of historical styles, including African rhythms, mournful Portuguese fado, and the music of indigenous groups. Samba, bossa nova and salsa are among the most famous Latin rhythms today.

Music from Rio

Portuguese fado music, which involves a vocal performance accompanied by the Portuguese guitar, was taken by settlers to Brazil in the 19th century. Rio de Janeiro soon produced an adaptation of this: a fairly quiet descendant called *choro*, typically with a trio of guitar, another stringed instrument, and flute, clarinet or saxophone. In the favelas (shanty towns) of Rio, *choro* became a more syncopated (accented) rhythm, cross-fertilising with African, mainly Angolan, music styles. In the early 20th century, samba began to emerge from this as the music of Rio's famous Carnival.

Another style, bossa nova, emerged in the late 1950s and early 60s on the beaches and in the clubs of Rio. A smoother, slower rhythm than samba, it was invented by composer Antonio Carlos Jobim (1927–94). Jobim's song *Desafinado* was the first bossa nova hit for João Gilberto in 1957.

Bossa nova was later taken up by American jazz musicians. Stan Getz (1927–91) was one of the leading lights of this movement; the album *Getz/Gilberto* (1964) is one of the best of the genre.

must know

A good publication with many standard Latin tunes is Chuck Sher's *The Latin Real Book* (Sher Music, 1997).

A samba bassline

Track 33

Samba bassline

This example shows the typically fast, double-tempo bassline of samba. The last note of each bar eases the transition from one chord to the next. A simpler version of this would have just four notes to each bar, instead of eight.

A bossa nova bassline

Track 34

Bossa nova bassline

Track 34 has a bossa nova bass pattern derived from a typically slow beat called *baion* in Brazilian music. Once you have mastered this pattern, you could identify the chord sequences found in a couple of famous bossa nova songs such as Antonio Carlos Jobim's *Corcovado* or *The Girl from Ipanema*, and practise whole tunes like this.

Salsa and Cuban music

Salsa is actually a generic New York term for a mix of Cuban and Puerto Rican styles.

The main Cuban styles that will interest bass players are rumba and son, both of which have an underlying rhythm called a *clave* (key), which is played on two hardwood sticks. There are subtle, yet significant differences between the *claves*; for more information on this fascinating subject, read Carlos del Puerto's book *The True Cuban Bass*.

Rumba is both a form of music and a dance. There are three main versions: slow *yambú*; faster, more complex *guaguancó*; and frenetic *columbia*.

Son uses a bass instrument alongside the guitar, trumpet, clave, maracas and bongo drums. To learn how to play son properly would be the equivalent of taking a degree programme in real bass playing, with up to a year-long visit to the island needed to learn directly from the masters! However, for rather less commitment you can also learn by listening to some of the great Cuban bands, such as Irakere, Los Van Van, Cubanismo, Arturo Sandoval, NG La Banda and the Buena Vista Social Club recordings.

Son montuno bassline

Son montuno is the modern Afro-Cuban sound – a hybrid of son that includes instrumental solos. Track 35 has a typical bassline in this style.

A son montuno bassline

Track 35

Motown and Stax

These two American record labels were hugely influential in the 1960s, each signing up a stable of artists who helped to shape the history of R 'n' B, soul and other forms of popular music.

The Motown Sound

In 1959, Berry Gordy set up a new record company in Detroit with the intention of running it along similar lines to the other great business in that town: the car industry. He developed a musical production line based, in part, upon the principles of Henry Ford.

Throughout the 60s, Motown Records encouraged and developed great songwriters and songwriting teams: Norman Whitfield and Barrett Strong, William 'Smokey' Robinson, Brian Holland, Lamont Dozier and Edward Holland. The Motown Sound, as it became known, was essentially a style of soul music using a distinctive bassline with drums, tambourines and gospel-inspired singing.

Gordy hired Maxine Powell to teach his stars proper etiquette and comportment. Most of all, he

Track 36

Motown-style bassline

had a team of musicians who gave the foundation for each of the hits, and at the bottom of that edifice – holding it all up – was the great bassist James Jamerson (*see pages 154–5*).

Track 36 would be the kind of line that James Jamerson would play at Motown on either his Precision bass or double bass. The descending chromatic line in the first three bars is characteristic.

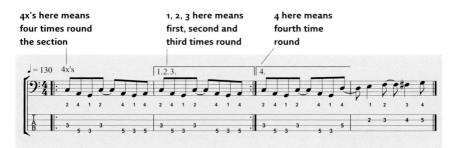

4x's here means
four times round
the section

1, 2, 3 here means
first, second and
third times round

4 here means
fourth time
round

Stax-style bassline

Stax Records

Track 37

Over at Stax, Jim Stewart and Estelle Axton had set up a label in Memphis in 1957, and were busy through the 60s and early 70s recording many of the great Memphis and Southern soul singers, such as Otis Redding, Wilson Pickett, Sam & Dave, Albert King and Rufus Thomas. The team of studio musicians there included Steve Cropper on guitar, Al Jackson on drums, Booker T. Jones on organ and Donald 'Duck' Dunn on bass.

Track 37 is in the style of a typical Duck Dunn bassline from the Stax period. Note the repetition of notes at root, fifth and sixth intervals. This is found a lot in the bass patterns that pushed along the early soul tunes.

Jazz

From its 19th-century origins in the American Deep South, jazz has developed into a host of sub-genres that play on the world stage today. Here, we look at a mere handful of jazz musicians who will be of special interest to the bass player.

Jazz bass players

The first bass instruments used in the early jazz of New Orleans were the brass tuba (bell pointing upwards) or sousaphone (bell pointing forwards), and the string bass. Later, in the 1920s, the bass saxophone was used – check out Adrian Rollini with Bix Beiderbecke on *At The Jazz Band Ball* (1924-8).

Pete Briggs played tuba with Louis Armstrong on some of the *Hot Fives* and *Hot Sevens* recordings (1925-8). Of the early string bass players, the best known were George 'Pops' Foster, who played with King Oliver and Louis Armstrong, and Wellman Braud, who played with Duke Ellington from 1926 to 1935. Listen to Braud playing on the Ellington re-mastered recordings on Naxos.

John Kirby doubled on tuba and double bass with the Fletcher Henderson Orchestra in the early 30s. He can be heard playing on the Columbia box set *A Study In Frustration*, which is available in many libraries but otherwise hard to find in the shops.

Walter Page was a great bassist who played with Count Basie's band in the late 30s and 40s. He was one of the best exponents of the walking bassline *(see page 100)* within the context of a big band, particularly with the Basie rhythm section of Freddie Green on guitar, Count Basie on piano and Jo Jones on drums. Eddie Jones later took over from Page in the Basie band, playing on the albums *April In Paris* (1955–6) and *The Atomic Mr. Basie* (1957).

One of the first jazz bass virtuosi was Jimmy Blanton, who joined Duke Ellington's band in 1939. He can be heard performing on *Pitter Panther Patter*, *Sepia Panorama* and *Jack The Bear*. Only a couple of years later, Blanton died of tuberculosis, aged 23. Nevertheless, he changed the course of jazz bass playing and inspired many of the players who came after him.

Bass player Milt Hinton was an inspiration for every musician from the 30s, when he first joined the jazz scene in Chicago, up until his death in 2000. He recorded with many of the greats in jazz, from Cab Calloway to Branford Marsalis.

Some more names in jazz...

Other jazz artists you should listen to include Charles Mingus (*Mingus Ah Um* and *Blues & Roots*), Paul Chambers (with Miles Davis and others), Scott LaFaro (*Bill Evans: Waltz For Debby* and *Sunday At The Village Vanguard*), Ray Brown (with Oscar Peterson and others), Ron Carter (*Miles Davis: E.S.P.* and *Miles Smiles*), Oscar Pettiford (with Lucky Thompson), Charlie Haden (*Ornette Coleman: Change Of The Century*), Dave Holland (*Miles Davis: In A Silent Way*), Glen Moore (Oregon), David Friesen and Christian McBride.

If that list seems like it covers pretty much the last 60 years of jazz, well, it's meant to. Happy hunting!

must know

Recommended recordings:
• Miles Davis, with Paul Chambers on bass: Relaxin' (Prestige, 1956), Kind Of Blue (Columbia, 1959)
• Duke Ellington: The Jimmy Blanton Era (Giants Of Jazz, 1990)
• Bill Evans, with Scott LeFaro on bass: Sunday At The Village Vanguard (Riverside, 1961), Waltz For Debby (Riverside, 1961)
• David Friesen, Glen Moore: Returning (Burnside, 1996)
• Christian McBride: Getting' To It (Verve, 1995)
• Jaco Pastorius: Metheny Bley Ditmas – Jaco (Jazz Door, 1974)
• Oscar Peterson, with Ray Brown on bass: Night Train (Verve, 1962), We Get Requests (1964)
• Oregon, with Glen Moore on bass: Crossing (ECM, 1985)

Walking basslines in jazz

Walking basslines are often used in jazz, where they may be improvised. They are steady, even rhythms that provide a smooth way of 'walking' through chord changes. Such basslines tend to move quite steadily up and down the tonal range. Three examples are shown below. They are also used in blues, R 'n' B, country and rockabilly music.

Chord names are marked above the stave for advanced students

Walking bassline – 1

Track 38

Walking bassline – 1

In Track 38 is a chord progression in the key of C. On each chord, first of all, we play the basic triad – root, third, fifth, third. This sounds a long way from a smooth walking line, but it gives the basic tones upon which to build.

Walking bassline – 2

Track 39

In Track 39 we have added one note to the triad – the second degree of each scale or mode. So it becomes root, second, third, fifth. This additional note has the

Walking bassline – 2

effect of smoothing out the line. It is also good if we can play all of this under the hand, as indicated by the fingering.

Walking bassline – 3

Track 40

Walking bassline – 3

In Track 40 we have added two more elements to the walking line mixture. It sounds relatively simple to the ear, but the theory behind it is quite complex.

In bars 1 and 2, we have root, second, third, fifth. We then come down using the Mixolydian mode. This can often be a useful approach when played over a II V progression on another instrument. (You will need to have gone beyond the beginner stage to understand these descriptions of chords.)

In bars 3 and 4, we have root, second, third, fifth and then a chromatic ascending line. Again, variations on any of these moves can be used over most chord progressions.

want to know more?
• One of the best books on jazz theory is Mark Levine's The Jazz Theory Book (Sher Music, 1995)
• A great book on walking bass is Ray Brown's Bass Method (Hal Leonard, 1999)
• Also, Mike Richmond's Modern Walking Bass Technique (Ped Xing Music, 1983)

weblinks
• Roughstock's History of Country Music at www.roughstock.com
• A listing of world music genres at http://worldmusiccentral.org

7 Bass theory

In previous chapters, we have explained elements of music theory as far as it was necessary to get you started with reading music and grasping the fundamentals of scales and different styles of music. In this section, we will delve deeper into the theory of music. We analyse the characteristics of that most common of scales – the major scale – and explain more about key signatures and intervals.

Understanding scales and keys

You already know that a scale goes up and down a series of notes in steps. What you may not have realised is that the steps are aurally uneven – despite looking even on a musical stave. Some steps are full tones while others are semitones. Here, as an example, we look at the pattern of steps on the major scale.

How the major scale works

To explain the basic theory behind scales, we will take the major scale as an example, and show how the pattern of tones and semitones affects the scale's key signatures.

Example 1 - C major

In Ex. 1 *(opposite)* is the C major scale, which by now should be very familiar to you. You will see that we have divided the notes into two four-note sets, called tetrachords (tetrachord comes from the Greek for four notes). The reason for this is because each four-note tetrachord is a pattern of tones. The intervals between the notes (ie the steps of the scale) are tone, tone, semitone (T, T, ST), separated by a tone, and then tone, tone, semitone (T, T, ST) again.

This is how every major scale is constructed: T, T, ST, T, T, T, ST. The pitches of the notes on the C major scale are CDEF in the first tetrachord and GABC in the second tetrachord. The semitone steps are from B to C and E to F. The rest are full tones.

Example 2 - G major

If we then take the second tetrachord of the C major scale (notes GABC) and put it lower down the stave,

The letters here indicate the tonal intervals, either tone (T) or semitone (ST)

These examples show us how the major scale is constructed. This is the simplest way to figure out exactly why and how we have key signatures.

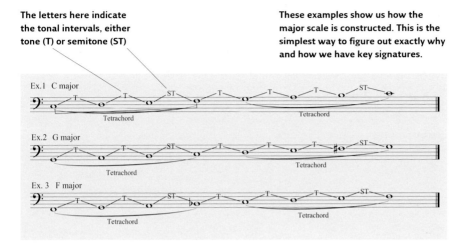

we have the first tetrachord of example 2 – that is, the first four notes of the G major scale.

We can then add another tetrachord on top, DEFG, to complete the scale. However, notice that to maintain the pattern of intervals (T, T, ST, T, T, T, ST), we have had to sharpen the F to F♯. This is how we get our first sharp key signature, G major (or 1 sharp). Easy, eh?

Example 3 – F major

In example 3, we go in the other direction. We've taken the bottom four notes of the C major scale, CDEF, and added a lower tetrachord, FGAB, to achieve a scale beginning and ending on F.

Again, to maintain the same pattern of tones and semitones (T, T, ST, T, T, T, ST), we have had to flatten the B to B♭. This is how we get our first flat key signature, F major (or 1 flat).

must know

If you are having trouble understanding the relationship between tones and semitones, look at a piano keyboard. There you will see that in every octave, two black keys appear to be 'missing' – ie two white keys sit side by side with no black key between them. The interval between such white keys is a semitone, whereas the interval between the other white keys is a full tone. The interval between a black and a white key is a semitone.

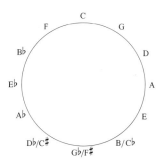

The cycle of fifths for the major scale helps you to identify the order and names of keys. Count clockwise from the top for sharps; anticlockwise for flats.

must know

The cycle of fifths is also called the cycle of fourths because it ascends in fourths going in the flat direction. This is useful to know because the bass is tuned in fourths. If you stay on one fret and go up in pitch – e.g. third fret, G, C, F, Bᵇ – you can see how the cycle works.

The cycle of fifths

Here we show a diagram that's common in music theory, called the cycle (or circle) of fifths. (It's called this because it moves in intervals of perfect fifths.) There are many variations of this diagram – we've shown it in a simple form for the major scales.

The C major scale has no sharps or flats and is placed at the top of the circle.

Counting round anticlockwise from the top gives you the order of flat key signatures: F, Bᵇ, Eᵇ, Aᵇ, Dᵇ, Gᵇ, Cᵇ. You can memorise this order with the mnemonic phrase: **F**at **B**oys **E**at **A**ll **D**ad's **G**reen **C**heese.

Counting round clockwise from the top gives you the order of sharp key signatures: G, D, A, E, B, F♯, C♯. You can memorise this order with the phrase: **G**ood **D**ays **A**lways **E**nd **B**y **F**eeling **C**heerful.

Working out key signatures

The cycle of fifths can help you to work out the name of the key for a piece of music. So, for example, if the key signature has one flat in it, count one letter anticlockwise round from C, which gives you the F major key signature. If the key signature has two flats, count two letters anticlockwise, which gives you Bᵇ major; three flats will give you Eᵇ major; four – Aᵇ major; five – Dᵇ major; six – Gᵇ major; seven – Cᵇ major.

If the key signature has one sharp, count one letter clockwise round from C, which gives you G on the major scale; two sharps – D major; three – A major; four – E major; five – B major; six – F♯ major; seven – C♯ major.

See pages 127–9 for practical examples relating to the order of sharps and flats in a key signature.

Understanding intervals

An interval is the distance in pitch between two notes. We've simply named the intervals on some of the scales and exercises in previous chapters. Now it's time to look closer at how intervals actually work in music theory.

Perfect, major and minor intervals

In Chapter 5 you met a variety of triads and arpeggios, which are sets of notes at specific intervals. For example, the intervals for the major triad on page 66 were stated as 'root, major third and perfect fifth'.

Intervals are so-named in reference to the notes of the scale they are on (second, third, fourth, fifth etc) and to their quality (perfect, major, minor, diminished or augmented).

Track 41

Perfect, major and minor intervals

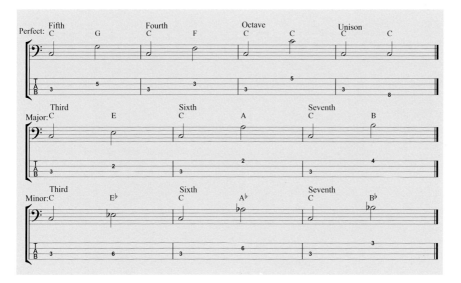

Notes at set intervals can be played sequentially, as is typical on the bass guitar (shown in the triad and arpeggio examples in Chapter 5), or they can be played simultaneously, as you would hear a chord played on a piano or guitar.

Track 41 demonstrates the perfect, major and minor intervals in the key of C major.

Perfect intervals on the major scale

The perfect intervals in the major scale are the distances from the root to the fourth, fifth and octave. Intervals are always counted in a way that includes the original note. So, C to F is a perfect fourth and C to G is a perfect fifth. C to C is an octave, and so the two notes are of the same pitch and are called a 'unison'.

Major intervals on the major scale

Following on from this, the major intervals in a major scale are the distances from the root to the third, sixth and seventh notes. Thus, C to E is a major third; C to A is a major sixth; C to B is a major seventh.

Track 42

Diminished and augmented intervals

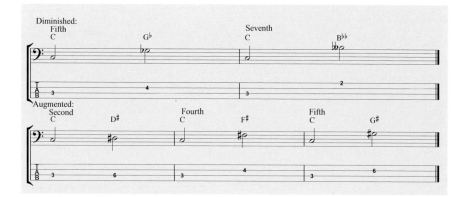

Minor intervals on the major scale

A major interval can be changed to a minor interval, usually by lowering the top note by a semitone. Thus, C to E♭ is a minor third; C to A♭ is a minor sixth; C to B♭ is a minor seventh.

Often, in jazz theory, we would also call these a flat 3, a flat 6 and a flat 7. Each term has its place in theory.

Diminished and augmented intervals

Track 42 has the commonest diminished (flattened) and augmented (sharpened) intervals. The naming of these, or indeed any, intervals often depends on context. The notes sound the same, but the intervals have different names because the context of the music may lead you to talk about a minor 6th rather than an augmented 5th, or vice versa.

Common diminished intervals

The two commonest diminished intervals are the diminished fifth, C to G♭, and the diminished seventh, C to B♭♭ (this is called B double flat). The diminished fifth is also commonly called the flat 5.

Common augmented intervals

The most common augmented intervals are the augmented second, C to D♯, the augmented fourth, C to F♯, and the augmented fifth, C to G♯. These can also be called sharp 2, sharp 4 and sharp 5.

The augmented second is most commonly found as the distance from the flat 6 to the sharp 7 of the harmonic minor scale. The augmented fourth sounds identical to the diminished fifth, and the augmented fifth also sounds identical to the minor sixth.

want to know more?
• Music theory is a big subject, so aim to learn a little each day alongside your physical practice on the bass guitar
• Make up your own mnemonic phrases for the order of keys if you want – usually the sillier they are, the more memorable
• The best book for basic theory is the AB Guide to Music Theory Vol 1 (Eric Taylor, 1989)
• Volume 2 in the same series is also good

weblinks
• For music theory on the internet, check www.icmp.uk.com
• Look up music theory on www.amazon.com for hundreds of other specialist titles

8 Basic practice

In this section, we will take you, slowly and gently, from being a non-reading musician to being a confident reader of basic rhythms. Remember that the concept of being a sight reader is mostly about reading patterns that you have already seen.

A simple rhythm on open strings

Let's start with something simple – playing a steady four-beat rhythm using quarter, half and whole notes on open strings, one string at a time.

---

must know

Refer to pages 46–51 if, at any time, you feel a need for a resumé of all the nuts and bolts of reading a piece of music – the order of notes on a stave, length of notes, basic terms and so on.

Playing on open strings

Each of the examples opposite are written to be played on an open string, so you do not have to worry about fingering for these exercises. Each bar consists of four beats – 1 2 3 4 – and, here, a quarter note is equal to a beat. A half note is equal to two beats, and a whole note is equal to four beats.

Play each of these open string examples with your metronome set to quarter note = 60 bpm (beats per minute). Take care to count, silently, four beats in each bar with the metronome. Make sure each note lasts for its full count. Although playing the notes here is easy, the important thing in these exercises is to maintain a steady rhythm and to feel comfortable keeping to that rhythm.

As well as playing the exercises by reading them on the page, you can play along with every example in this book with the CD provided. It's a good idea to play in both ways for comparison.

Track 43: open string exercise on the E string

Track 44: open string exercise on the A string

Track 45: open string exercise on the D string

Track 46: open string exercise on the G string

Tracks 43–6

Open string exercises

Understanding a score

Here we'll look a little deeper into the kind of information you're likely to encounter when reading a musical score, such as rehearsal letters, tied notes and repeat instructions.

More musical notation

The musical example opposite is, again, made up of quarter notes and half notes, but now we've also added quarter note rests. We'll also be looking at several new concepts: rehearsal letters; ties; and two different ways of making a piece or section repeat.

Rehearsal letters

Letters (such as the A, B and C you can see in our example) are placed at points in a piece of music where changes occur, and often where a verse or chorus begins. A band leader or musical director can then refer the musicians quickly to the relevant section in the piece. This saves rehearsal time and cuts out the need to always go back to the beginning after any mistakes. Very often bar numbers will be used with, or even instead of, rehearsal letters.

Ties

A tie is quite simply a curved line connecting two notes of the same pitch. The resulting note length is a combination of the two note values. There are two reasons why you would use tied notes rather than one note. The first is across a bar line; the second is within a bar to give value to a note that would be difficult or too confusing to write in any other way. So, at letter B, for example, the last quarter note of bar 9 is tied to the first quarter note of bar 10, giving a note length equal to a half note or two beats.

Two methods for repeating a section

Letter A is made up of four bars played twice. The first four bars have a double bar line at either end with two dots showing the section that we will repeat. The second time through section A we go from bar 3 to bar 5 and on to section B. The numbers over bars 4 and 5 indicate the bar to play on the first and second time through (in this case they are identical, but in other cases they might vary).

The letters D.C. at the end of the piece are an abbreviation for *Da Capo*, which is Italian for "go back to the beginning and play the whole thing again, stopping at the word *Fine*" (bar 14).

Track 47

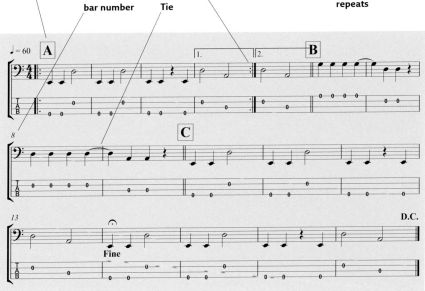

Rehearsal letter

bar number   Tie

Repeat symbol

Rehearsal letters, ties and repeats

Playing on the E and A strings

You will now practise playing notes on the first five frets of the E and A strings. You have only four playing fingers on your left hand, so you will need to shift your fingers during these exercises – make sure you follow the fingering patterns shown.

Notes and accidentals

The first line of music (Track 48) has all of the notes and accidentals used in exercises 1–4 (Tracks 49–52). The accidentals, if you remember, are the sharps, flats and naturalisations in a piece of music (*see page 48*). The effect of any accidental is only for one bar, unless it's used in a key signature.

Exercises 1–4

The first two exercises should be played on the E string. So, all the A notes will be played at the fifth fret. Exercises 3 and 4 should all be played on the A string. So, all the D notes here will be played at the fifth fret on the A string.

Finger-per-fret system

Beginners often play with only three fingers of the left hand, without the little finger. However, it is best to use all four fingers to keep your hand muscles balanced. The fingering patterns in these exercises use the 'finger-per-fret' system. This simply means that four fingers can cover four frets, or four semitones, at a time. When you need to cover more than four frets, as in these exercises, which cover five, you shift one of your fingers. Follow the fingering patterns shown to see how this works in practice.

must know

An alternative to playing with a 'finger-per-fret' is the typical double bass fingering, which uses the first, second and fourth fingers for three adjacent chromatic notes (eg, F, F#, G). This fingering can be useful on the lower reaches of the bass guitar. Often the two fingering systems will be used in the same piece of music to facilitate movement.

Tracks 48–52

Exercises on the E and A strings

Track 48: all of the notes and accidentals used in the exercises below

Tracks 49-50: two exercises on the E string

Tracks 51-2: two exercises on the A string

Playing on the D and G strings

You've worked with notes on the E and A strings. Now it's time to move on to the D and G strings. We'll also look at ways of shifting the hand position and choosing how to play the notes.

Notes on the D and G strings

The first line of music opposite shows two ways of looking at the notes on the first five frets of the D string and the G string. The position shift (moving the position of the fingering hand on the neck of the guitar) can either be made by moving the first finger from D$^\sharp$ to E or by moving the fourth finger from F$^\sharp$ to G. Which move is best will depend on the context of the notes in the piece you are playing.

Exercises 1-4

The first two exercises should be played on the D string. Be careful to use a finger-per-fret, making sure that the fingertips are placed just behind the frets. This will make the tone of each note much better and eliminate any buzzes or rattles from your playing. Your fingertips should be able to feel the fret-wire, and that makes it easier to concentrate on reading the music too.

Now look at exercises 3 and 4. You will see that each of them has a position shift at some point in the music. This means that you still keep the left hand hovering over the strings, with each of the four fingers ready to play one of the notes. We've indicated which finger to use under the music.

This approach is very different to the tablature, which is also given, because eventually you will be

Tracks 53-7

Exercises on the D and G strings

making your own fingering decisions. Tablature permanently ties you in to the hand position that the transcriber of any music has used.

Track 53: two comparative bars for the D string and for the G string: they show different ways of writing the same notes and offer variations for the fingering and position shift

Tracks 54-5: two exercises on the D string

Tracks 56-7: two exercises on the G string

Getting a feel for rhythm

Now you will play a more rhythmic piece using notes on all four strings up to the fifth fret. Here we are going to use our knowledge of scales and scale fingerings to help us stay in position and make the job of reading music slightly easier.

must know

On the bass guitar, the important thing to remember is not the key, but the fingering of the scale. See pages 54-5 for the major scale fingering which we are employing with these exercises.

Eyes on notes, fingers on strings

Most people, when they start reading rhythms in music, will use almost the same techniques as when they started reading books. That is, they place their index finger under the notes and try to figure out the sound by following the line along. And, just as this would fail to impress any employer if you did it with a book, it is also fairly redundant as a means of reading music. Especially when you need to keep both hands on the instrument. So just keep your eyes on the music and your hands in position on the bass.

Some points about rhythm

Usually, a bar in 4/4 time will be subdivided into eighth notes using the counting system: 1 *and* 2 *and* 3 *and* 4 *and* (see the rhythm example in Track 58).

This is fine, but it doesn't really help us to place the notes 'physically' in tempo. You'll see that the notation for Track 58 has metronome markings placed above the notes (the down and up beats). By now, you should have a good electronic metronome – one that sounds like a clockwork metronome, but differs from it by not limping or slowing down.

The metronome will give you the basic beat. Now, to find exactly where the *and* of each beat should be placed, you can first of all double up the metronome

Rhythm example
with down and up
symbols

Track 58

setting. So, 60 beats per minute will become 120
bpm. This is an imperfect solution, however, as you'll
soon find that, at faster tempos, the rate of beats
tapping out of the metronome will drive you crazy.

Finding the 'and' of the beat

The really hip way of doubling up the metronome
speed is to leave it at the indicated speed, which,
in this case, is 60 bpm, and start counting with an
and on the first click. Like this: *and* 1 *and* 2 *and* 3
and 4 *and*. This will have two effects. The
metronome will sound like a snare drum playing
on the off-beat and, as a consequence, the music
will start to swing more.

Another good method to help you subdivide the
beat into eighth notes, is to move one of your feet up
and down with the metronome, keeping the heel on
the floor. By this, I don't mean tap your foot,
however. If you tap your shoe, trainer or boot, this
very quickly takes over from the metronome and
your tempos will rapidly start to wander.

Instead, gently move the foot up and down with
the beat. When the foot is on the floor, that's the
beat. When the foot is in the air, that's the *and* of the
beat. The nice thing about using this system is that

Fingering exercises

Tracks 59–60

you really can physically feel the *and* of the beat. This comes in particularly handy with syncopated, or off-beat, eighth notes, which you'll meet later.

Try out all of these counting methods in conjunction with exercises 1 and 2 above, and see which one suits you the best.

Using scale fingerings

As with the previous examples, you should use a finger-per-fret. This fingering of the major scale can be used anywhere on the neck of the bass guitar. Whatever the key of the piece of music you are reading, just place the second finger on the root of the scale and all of the notes will be under the hand. This also means that you can concentrate on the music and not ever have to look at your hand.

must know

You may have noticed that over these first reading practices, we've been introducing note names that don't commonly crop up in music. $C^\flat$, $B^\sharp$, $F^\flat$ and $E^\sharp$ all exist – usually in key signatures with six or seven sharps or flats.

Fingering exercises 1 and 2

The first piece (Track 59) is short and was written to show you how to use this fingering system. I've written which fingers to use under the music.

The second piece (Track 60) is in the key of C, so use exactly the same fingering system.

Playing beyond the 5th fret – 1

So far in this chapter you have played notes using a mix of open strings and the first five frets on the neck of the bass. Now you will be shifting your left hand position along the neck to play notes at the 5th to 8th frets on the E and A strings. You will also practise straight and swung eighth notes.

Goodbye to open strings

In this section, we will not be going anywhere near the open strings. Open strings have their place and are very useful at times, particularly when you're trying to emulate the sound of a double bass on the bass guitar with 'rakes', 'skips' and 'dead notes'. You will always be able to use open strings, but not, from now on, as musical reference points to help you find your position on the neck.

Notes beyond the 5th fret

First of all, let's see which notes are going to be available to us at this part of the bass neck. Play Track 61 and place your first finger on the fifth fret of the E string. Using a finger per fret, play the four notes under the hand going up the string. They are: A, A♯, B, C – or, to put it another way: A, B♭, B, C.

Now do the same thing on the A string. Playing from the fifth fret, and using a finger-per-fret, gives us: D, D♯, E, E♯ – or D, E♭, E, F.

Track 61

Notes beyond the 5th fret

Eighth note exercises

Tracks 62-3

Eighth note exercises

Exercise 1 (Track 62) is played with eighth notes at the 5th to 8th frets. It should sound like a piece of folk music – check out any of the albums by Fairport Convention, from Liege & Lief onwards, to hear examples of British folk music, or The Chieftains for Irish folk music.

Exercise 2 (Track 63) is played with swung eighth notes. Swing or swung time is when the beat is subdivided into a triplet rather than two equal eight notes. This is more typical of jazz time than heavy metal pumping straight eight notes. Compare the difference in sound between Tracks 62 and 63. Also, if you can get hold of it, listen to Will Lee's bassline on *Walk Between the Raindrops* (from *The Nightfly*, 1982, Donald Fagen, Warner Bros. Records), which is an excellent example of a swung bass guitar part.

must know

Notating any degree of feel or swing in written music is very difficult. Sometimes a swung phrase will be written as a series of dotted eighth notes plus sixteenth notes, but usually it is written as straight eighths with an implied 'triplet feel'.

Playing beyond the 5th fret - 2

Following on from the last practice, we're staying at the fifth fret and adding the notes on the D and G strings. Again, we'll be exploring the notes readily available under the hand.

Life at the fifth fret

In Track 64, using a finger per fret from the fifth fret on the D string gives us: G, G♯, A, A♯ - or, to look at it another way: G, A♭, A, B♭. Playing from the fifth fret on the G string gives us C, C♯, D, D♯ - or C, D♭, D, E♭.

Now that we've learnt all of the notes under the hand at the fifth fret from the E string to the G string, let's try some music that covers all four strings.

Track 65 (Ex.1) is meant to be a slow, funky piece of music. We've added some expression marks to it as well as placing the fingerings under the notes. The

Tracks 64-5

Notes on the D and G strings, and an exercise on all the strings

first bar has a legato mark (–) over the C. It means that you should play the note as long as possible in the time alloted to it. The D♭ has an accent over it (>). This means that you should place a slight emphasis on the note.

The life of a working musician

You've just finished a gig playing 1930s-style music on the double bass; it's 2.30am and there's a long drive home ahead. Get home, unload car, set the alarm for 7am, sleep, leave house at 8am, drive to studio for 9am, tune bass guitar, check first piece to be recorded: a selection from *West Side Story*. Finish session at 2.30pm, drive to next gig, play from 8pm, covering tunes from 1950 to the present day. Finish at midnight, drive home, set alarm for 8am ... And that's about as busy as it gets.

For those of you who are still not sure about learning to read music, the itinerary above from an ordinary day will either put you off for life or set you practising every piece of music you can get your hands on. In one 24-hour period, you can be called upon to read music for waltzes from the 1890s, the latest download hits, classical music of all styles (from Bach to Bernstein), ethnic music (from Jewish and Iranian to Irish folk and Cockney sing-alongs), and jazz standards (from Louis Armstrong to Joe Zawinul). As a professional musician, you're expected to be able to play covers of every kind of music – punk tunes, Stravinsky, the Moroccan National Anthem ...

Memorising the keys

We've come a long way in the last few pages, but until the notes, key signatures and the order of sharps and flats are second nature to you, you'll always struggle with your playing. In earlier chapters we introduced you to some mnemonic phrases – now see if you can put theory into practice.

The key to remembering

We've looked at various fingering positions on the neck of the bass and the notes that can be found under the hand up to the eighth fret. So now, when you scan a piece of music, you should be able to check the range of the notes and the key signature, and then place your hand in a position that will cover all or most of the notes in the piece.

But how do you figure out from the key signature exactly which sharps or flats apply to the tune you're trying to read? Well, it's true that you could simply read their position on the stave, but it's far easier and considerably quicker to use memory joggers such as the ones you met in Chapters 4 and 7.

For example, the cycle of fifths *(see page 106)* can help you recognise the key signature and order of sharps or flats. You can also put to good use the mnemonic phrases, or memory joggers, that have been mentioned.

For example, **F**at **B**oys **E**at **A**ll **D**ad's **G**reen **C**heese gives you the order of flat key signatures on the major scale. **G**ood **D**ays **A**lways **E**nd **B**y **F**eeling **C**heerful gives you the order of sharp key signatures on the major scale.

Four examples of sharps and flats on a key signature

Key signature recognition

Track 66

Four key signature examples

In the notation at the top of the page are four different key signatures. If you count the number of sharps or flats on each key signature, then refer to the cycle of fifths on page 106, you can see what the keys are called on the major scale.

- Ex. 1 has seven sharps, so it is in the key of C♯ major
- Ex. 2 has seven flats, so it is in the key of C♭ major
- Ex. 3 has five sharps, so it is in the key of B major
- Ex. 4 has four flats, so it is in the key of A♭ major

The order of sharps and flats on the stave

As well as knowing how to identify a key signature simply from the number of sharps or flats in it, you should also learn the order of sharps and flats as they are written on the stave. (Don't confuse this with the order of flats and sharps on the cycle of fifths.)

Mnemonic for the order of sharps on the stave

A popular mnemonic for the order of sharps is **F**ather **C**harles **G**oes **D**own **A**nd **E**nds **B**attle.

If you look again at Ex. 1, which uses all seven possible sharps, you will see that the order of those sharps on the stave follows the order of first letters in the mnemonic phrase – F, C, G, D, A, E, B.

Mnemonic for the order of flats

You simply reverse the phrase to get the order of flats on the stave: **B**attle **E**nds **A**nd **D**own **G**oes **C**harles' **F**ather. Ex. 2 uses all seven flats.

This reversible mnemonic works in exactly the same way for the bass and treble clefs.

Caught in a tight spot?

By now, you're possibly thinking that you've got this key signature business cracked. Then, someone gives you a sheet of music with five sharps on it (Ex. 3). Your mind is a blank – you can't remember which key has five sharps on the circle of fifths. Okay, try this: **F**ather **C**harles **G**oes **D**own **A**nd – this makes the last sharp in the key signature an A$^\sharp$. Raise the A$^\sharp$ by a semitone and that gives you the key: B major.

The process is slightly more complicated for flats. Four flats in Ex. 4? **B**attle **E**nds **A**nd **D**own. Go back one, and that gives you A$^\flat$ major.

Track 66

In Ex. 5 is a piece of music which is played on Track 66. It has five flats on the key signature. What key is it in?

A tip for this piece: place your second finger on the root of the scale, then you will find that all of the notes can be comfortably played under the hand.

want to know more?

The following books are very good for reading practice:
• Rich Appleman: Reading Contemporary Electric Bass (1983, Berklee Press)
• For rhythm reading, try Louis Bellson: Modern Reading Text in 4/4 (1963, Belwin Mills)
• Carol Kaye: Electric Bass Lines Complete Vols. 1 & 2 (Alfred)

weblinks
• www.bassbooks.com
• www.jazzwise.com

9 Advanced practice

In this section of the book, we will look at more advanced concepts and notation, including rhythms that include sixteenth notes. Every rhythmic grouping will be demonstrated on the CD. There is also a short section at the end to show you how to read swung or jazz rhythms.

Sixteenth-note patterns

In the previous chapter, we concentrated on subdivisions of the beat from whole notes to eighth notes. In this Advanced chapter, we're going to look at sixteenth-note patterns, which can be played and written in a number of ways.

Rhythmic groupings

There are two sixteenth notes to each eighth note and four to the quarter note. It's a good idea to familiarise yourself with the sound and feel of the rhythmic groupings used in sixteenth-note rhythms. We've listed these in Example 1, below (Track 67).

Two eighth notes have been included with these groupings, which will be useful as a reference point. Eighth notes crop up a lot in sixteenth-note patterns. Play each of the groups in Example 1 as a whole bar of 4/4 – that is, play four identical groups in each bar. To get used to the sound and feel of them at different tempos, play each pattern at tempos from quarter note = 60 bpm up to quarter note = 112 bpm. Do the same with Examples 2a and 2b (Track 68)

Tracks 67–8

Rhythmic groupings

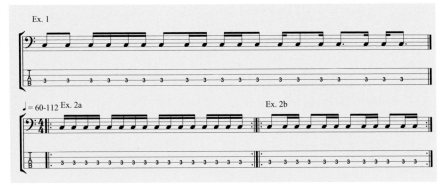

Imitate a drummer

Very often, you will hear teachers and students using this system of subdividing the beat into sixteenth notes: 1-e-an-a, 2-e-an-a, 3-e-an-a, 4-e-an-a.

However, this system has a tendency to slow down students' recognition of patterns. Also, it's quite a mouthful at anything but the slowest tempos. There is an easier way to place notes in sixteenth-note bass patterns. That is to quietly make the sound that a drummer would make on his hi-hat cymbals when playing continuous sixteenths. It sounds something like *Ta*-ka-ti-ka, *Ta*-ka-ti-ka etc., with a slight emphasis on the first syllable of each group of four. This system will be particularly useful in the next group of exercises.

Stab phrasing in funk playing

Once you have become used to the groups above, we can go on to some of the 'stab phrasing' – chords played with force – commonly used in funk playing. These phrases can be played on the bass, and similar phrases can be heard in many top brass sections (listen to *The Very Best of Earth, Wind and Fire* for some good examples). You'll see in Ex. 3, overleaf (Track 69) that they all have articulation marks below them. The v-shaped ones indicate more attack.

In order to understand fully these groupings, subdivide the beat into four sixteenths. You'll see that the first group consists of the 2nd and 4th sixteenths, the second is just the fourth sixteenth, and so on. The last three groups have *legato* and *staccato* marks under them. This means that you should play them 'long-short', which would sound like 'doo-dat'. On the CD, we have placed these

must know

If you have a drum machine, it would be a good idea to programme it with the patterns in the exercises and examples here, and then listen to them played that way first at different tempos.

Ex. 3

Nine examples of beat subdivisions

Track 69

groupings on the last beat of the second bar. The best way to learn how to play them is to make each of them the last beat of a bar of 4/4. This can be done by playing along with a drum machine, if you have one. Use the sounds that we've given above, and that will help to place the syncopated phrasing, particularly the last sixteenth of the bar.

Rests and ties

So, now these groupings and short phrases can be combined with rests and ties to create funky sixteenth-note basslines (Track 70). Look at Ex. 4c. If you analyse the rhythm, you'll see that it breaks down into 16-8, 16-8, 16-8, 16-8, 16-16-8. It's similar to that familiar tune at the beginning of adverts at the cinema (which, incidentally, was recently used in sampled form as the basis of a dance hit). Ex. 4d is a typical funk pattern from the 1970s.

Track 70

Funky basslines with rests and ties

Phrases with ties

In the first part of Advanced Practice, we looked at various ways of subdividing the beat into sixteenth notes. Included at the end of that section were a few one bar phrases that included ties. So, how on earth do you read, count or even feel those things?

The Charleston rhythm

Let's see how those tied notes work with one short phrase: a dotted eighth note followed by a sixteenth note. At a quarter note = 80 bpm, this simple rhythm can sound like the opening phrase of a dance from the 1920s: the Charleston.

If you've never heard of this dance, then maybe a trip to your local record library would unearth some good examples. Ask the librarians to order a version of *The Charleston* by The Pasadena Roof Orchestra for you, if they don't have it on the shelves.

Exercise 1

In the notation for Track 71, we've indicated three versions of the same phrase. The second is tied to an eighth note and the third is tied to a quarter note. These additions make the second part of the phrase longer, but the basic phrase remains the same.

Track 71

Variations of a simple phrase

Variation on a 'Charles-ton' rhythm

Track 72

Exercises 2a and 2b

Ex. 2a (Track 72) shows our 'Charles-ton' rhythm tied to an eighth note. The eighth note is connected to another eighth note; this one falls on the 'and' of beat two. It's then followed by a quarter note on beat three. So you can combine the 'Charles-ton' sounding rhythm with a normal eighth note count to give you the phrase: 'Charles-ton and three'.

Ex. 2b is the same phrase as 2a, but written as two bars of 'cut common time', which is often used in notation for older forms of jazz, and samba. Some people find it easier to read cut common time rather than double-tempo sixteenth notes.

Another varation on a 'Charles-ton' rhythm

Track 73

Exercises 3a and 3b

This example (Track 73) has our dotted eighth/sixteenth pairing tied to a sixteenth/eighth/sixteenth grouping, followed by a quarter note.

Again, example 3b shows how it would look when written in cut common time.

Hill Street Blues-style phrase

Exercises 4a and 4b

Track 74 is a variation on Ex. 2a, with the 'and' of beat two tied to beat three. For those of you who can remember it, this is like the opening phrase of the theme music for the 1980s American television show *Hill Street Blues*.

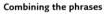

Combining the phrases

Exercise 5

Now it's time to put this together in one piece. Track 75 includes a combination of some of the phrases shown in this section.

More sixteenth-note patterns

Here we're going to look at some more subdivisions of the quarter note. In time, you'll become more and more familiar with the various ways in which a quarter note can be divided, and so start to instantly recognize common rhythmic patterns.

Sight reading

Many students worry whether reading on gigs will involve music that can't be played without practice. This is very rarely the case. Most reading situations involve checking the geography of the piece quickly and then playing after the count in or on the down beat. Most commercial music contains rhythms and patterns that you will have seen and heard many times before. It's *how* you play them that matters.

So, hopefully, all this reading business – and its necessity – is beginning to make sense to you. Now take a deep breath, because here comes some more information on sixteenth notes and ties.

Track 76

A rhythm like a cantering horse; Ex.1b is the same rhythm in cut common time

Exercise 1 – Track 76

Let's take a look at two similar subdivisions of the quarter note. This example shows an eighth note followed by two sixteenths played as a bar of 4/4. The sound of this pattern is very much like the noise that a horse's hooves make when cantering.

Exercise 2 - Track 77

Here the previous pattern is reversed: two sixteenths followed by an eighth note. Again, example 2b shows how it would look in cut common time.

The reversed pattern

Exercise 3 - Track 78

Now comes the interesting part. If we tie these two groups together, as in example 3a, we end up with a syncopation that subdivides the first two beats into sixteenths in the following way: 3 3 2.

Counting the sixteenth notes, the emphasis would be **1** (2) **3**, **1** (2) **3**, **1** (2). Try clapping and then playing this pattern against a metronome set to a quarter note = 80 bpm. Example 3b gives the same rhythm in cut common time.

Exercise 4 - Track 79

Here we've linked the pattern that we've just learnt with one that we looked at on page 136 *(Ex.2a)*.

Linking patterns together

Vocalising written rhythms

This can be a source of embarrassment or laughter, but the method of approximating the sounds of the bass guitar with one or two short, rhythmic vocal sounds is a useful one. It can be employed to sing the rhythms of any difficult bass part.

Time to express yourself

On page 133, we described one method of singing along with the hi-hat rhythm that a drummer would typically play for a sixteenth-note rhythm. Another method which was developed for singing along with the boogaloo rhythms of the 1960s and early 70s involved the following sounds: either 'Guh' and 'Goh'/'Gong', or 'Duh' and 'Dah'.

Try vocalising these sounds while playing Ex. 1a (Track 80; Ex. 1b shows how the rhythm looks, and sounds, in cut common time.)

Now try your vocal method on the same rhythm that you had on page 134 – it's similar to the Pearl & Dean advertisements from the movies (Track 81; Ex. 2a and 2b in cut common time).

Tracks 80-81

Two vocal exercises

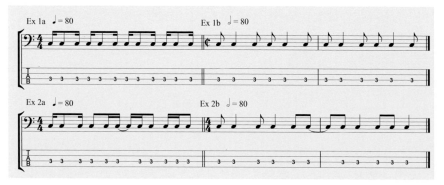

Ex 1a ♩ = 80   Ex 1b ♩ = 80

Ex 2a ♩ = 80   Ex 2b ♩ = 80

By now, you'll either be getting more comfortable with this concept or, more likely, have tears of laughter pouring down your face. In either case, persevere with this vocal rhythm system and I'm sure that eventually you will find it very useful. With a bit of practice, it can even be made to sound quite hip.

A short funky riff

One of the problems with any rhythm reading method is matching a change in pitch with the changing rhythm. So, let's try playing the rhythm we've just practised as a riff over a short funky sequence in the key of C (Track 82).

As you can see below, the piece looks complicated, but by using vocal sounds that begin with either 'Duh' or 'Guh' (whichever you prefer), you can make a good approximation of the part before having a go at playing it.

must know
Try out this vocalising method on basslines in other books you might have on bass guitar. Carol Kaye's Electric Bass Lines Complete Vols. 1 & 2 would be a great source for this.

Track 82

A funky riff

More sixteenth-note variations

Here we'll return to some sixteenth-note rhythms, so let's look at more variations in the way that the quarter note can be divided. It all helps to build up a palette of familiar rhythms.

Exercises 1 and 2

The first example below (Track 83) shows a bar of quarter notes subdivided into dotted eighth notes tied to sixteenth notes. Play the rhythm at the tempo indicated to give yourself a chance to feel the subdivisions of the beat. If you play this exercise at a faster pace – about a quarter note = 124 bpm – it will sound like the shuffle rhythm much used by Status Quo ... and every boogie band before and since them.

Exercise 1b shows the same rhythm written in cut common time.

The pattern reversed

Ex. 2a (Track 84) shows this pattern reversed – that is, a sixteenth note tied to a dotted eighth note.

In Ex. 2b, we've written it two different ways in long form to show how it sounds.

Tracks 83–4

More sixteenth-note exercises

Putting it all together

Now let's try combining these two new additions to our rhythmic palette in a heavy little ditty in C minor:

A C minor bassline

Track 85

Becoming a better musician

If you're still wondering why you should be putting yourself through the mill to learn how to read music, just think about the benefits that come from being a bass player who can read notation. You'll be able to play any piece of music, in any clef, without struggling with an incomplete and often confusing tablature. People will ring you for gigs having total confidence in your abilities. You'll be able to add ever more music to your repertoire quickly, do sessions, play with orchestras or big bands.

Put quite simply, you'll be a better musician.

Swing and jazz rhythms

This introduction to jazz rhythms will include some complex concepts. Whether or not jazz is to your taste, learning about jazz rhythms is a good way to advance your experience on bass.

Getting a feel for jazz

From time to time, you may find yourself in situations where you are asked to read bass parts that include swing or jazz rhythms. It could be in a big band, either at school or in one of the many excellent bands that are set up around the world by musicians wishing to play music that is more testing than their usual gigs. It could be while playing in a small jazz ensemble with friends, or when your band is called on to back a singer.

With jazz even more so than with most other types of music, it really pays to know the subject, and that starts with listening *(see opposite)*. However, it is possible to learn what an arranger or composer intended through the written music that sits in front of you waiting to be played. So, let's take a look at some of the concepts involved in writing jazz rhythms. To do this in the easiest way possible, we'll adapt some of the themes we've already come across.

A typical quarter-note walking bassline would look like the example below (Track 86).

Track 86

Walking bassline based on the F major scale

This indicates that the piece should be played 'swung'

This bassline (Ex. 1) is based on the notes of the F major scale. Note the indication above the stave that the piece should be played 'swung'. Even though there are no eighth notes in this example, the subdivision of each beat is into a quarter/eighth triplet. Bear that in mind and you should find that the line can be made to swing. Listen to the track on the CD to help pick up the feel of a swinging rhythm.

The chord symbols below the stave are based on the progression II, V, I ,VI in the key of F major.

Listening as a learning tool

The first thing that I'll say on this subject probably sounds quite obvious and even a little harsh. It's not possible to play jazz, or any style of music, for that matter, successfully until you've listened to it thoroughly. By that I mean lots of it, from every era, from the 1920s and 30s right through to the present day. There is nothing worse than trying to play 40s-style jazz music with someone whose listening does not extend further back than the jazz of the 1960s. Equally, playing with someone whose listening finished in the 40s, or 50s, can be a curious experience. Believe me, some of those people still think The Beatles were the worst thing to happen to popular music.

Another walking bassline in F

Track 87

For these exercises, it is perfectly all right to use open strings. That is because we are trying to produce as closely as possible the sound of a double bass, and the looseness of open strings helps. If you have access to a double bass, so much the better.

Another walking bassline in F – Track 87

This is a more chromatic version of Ex. 1. ('chromatic' denotes a scale of semitones). This will give you the slightly harder task of trying to decide which fingers should be used for the notes outside of the major scale. You can either use the system of a-finger-per-fret, which will cover most of the notes easily, or use a combination of that plus double bass fingering (fingers 1, 2 and 4 of the fretting hand).

A student of the bass working through some advanced exercises

Playing a walking bassline using the finger-per-fret system. Note that the hand is spread out but not too stiff.

The usual rule for ascending and descending chromatic lines is to write sharps for ascending lines and flats for the corresponding descending line. And, yes, the author has broken that rule in bar 2, because the E♭ and E relate to the flat 3 and 3 of the C7 chord.

Exercise 3 – Track 88

Here is another short piece, this time based on chords II, V, I, VI, in the key of B♭ major. This time I've inserted some eighth note skips. I usually tell students not to play any skips at all when first learning to play walking basslines. The tendency for a beginner is to put too many skips and triplet figures into walking lines, which can end up sounding like Irish jigs. Not that there's anything at all wrong with an Irish jig; it's just that jigs and jazz don't tend to sit well together. For those of you who would like to hear jazz and Gaelic music played together perfectly, try listening to the immaculate piano playing of Micheál O'Súilleabháin.

must know

one of the best books for learning about reading and playing walking basslines is Modern Walking Bass Technique Vol.1 by Mike Richmond (Ped Xing Music). Your local music shop should be able to order it for you.

Track 88

A B♭ major bassline with 'skip'

Reading jazz rhythms

Here are a few more concepts involved in reading jazz rhythms, including samples of some of the different ways in which you can transcribe the same piece of music.

Key factors in writing music

The first concept when it comes to notating music is that it is not possible, or even desirable, to write out everything exactly as you mean it to be played. The second concept is that you should always try to write out a rhythm using the least amount of information needed to make it logical and playable. These ideas are demonstrated in Examples 1, 2 and 3, opposite.

These examples show different versions of the same basic theme. Example 1 is the most usual way to write out a typical eighth-note swing, or bebop, rhythm. As you can see, it involves writing out only eight notes, plus *tenuto* (held or lengthen) and *staccato* (shorten) marks. It's simple to write and, more importantly, simple to read. The decision on how much to swing the piece of music is left to the player.

The two eighth notes at the end of a phrase that are indicated to be played long-short give us the typical jazz sound, which is best translated as 'be-bop' (hence the be-bop genre), or 'doo-dat'.

Variations
Sometimes, the same phrase will be written out as in example 2. This involves writing more information on the stave – using dotted eighth notes and sixteenth notes. This is often the way that phrases were written out in earlier forms of jazz.

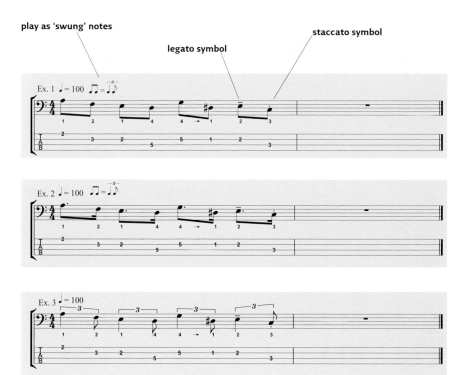

play as 'swung' notes

legato symbol

staccato symbol

Three ways of writing
the same music

Track 89

Strictly speaking, the most complete and correct version of this piece of music is Example 3. But this involves writing and reading so much information on the stave that it would soon become overly complicated – particularly as, ordinarily, you'd be given pages of this kind of music to read. Curiously enough, though, this form would be the best way to write jazz rhythms for classical string players (violins, violas and cellos).

As you can see from these three examples, the underlying concept is that the beat is subdivided into a subtle 'triplet feel'.

Handling syncopated beats

Students often struggle with the idea of syncopated rhythms – that is, rhythms that don't adhere to the regular beat of the time signature. But so much popular music of at least the last 50 years has been immersed in syncopation that it is, perhaps, easier to pick it up intuitively – as a feeling more than a concept.

The offbeat

I suspect that many of you are still puzzled by the syncopated swung rhythms that you can come across in bass charts. That is, the kind of rhythms that either anticipate the beat or are played after the beat. These phrases are very often played in unison with other instruments, which makes it all the more important that they're played correctly.

A simple way of showing whether the notes should fall on the beat or off the beat can be to use a method that we've already looked at earlier on in the Advanced Practice part of the book – namely tapping your foot. While I wouldn't recommend that you do this all the time when you're playing, it can be an

Track 90

A syncopated rhythm

excellent method for analysing both straight and swung rhythms.

Start by tapping your foot in time to a metronome – not too fast, or the Achilles tendon and calf muscles will rapidly complain. When your foot is on the floor, that's the downbeat; when it's in the air, that's the offbeat. If you have a succession of offbeat eighth notes, play them each time the foot is in the air. In this case, also play them swung.

Keeping hold of the beat

The example opposite shows as many variations on this theme as possible. Try to resist the trap of playing notes that are meant to be on the beat as syncopated rhythms, and vice versa. This is a common error among players at all levels.

The example given is based on the chords of the harmonised C major scale. While keeping the notes simple, we've deliberately changed the rhythms in each bar to give you practice at offbeat eighth-note phrasing.

want to know more?
- **There is an excellent book in the Sher Music series called The Real Easy Book Level 1 (Bass Clef), which includes 42 jazz and Latin tunes with melodies written in the bass clef, plus chord information and a sample bassline.**
- **The best way to further advance your music reading skills is to get hold of as many other scores as you can find.**

weblinks
- **www.bassbooks.com**
- **www.jazzwise.com**

10 Great bass players

In this section, we will look at the styles of some of the great bass players, both on bass guitar and on double bass. The reason for doing this is to motivate you to listen to as many styles as possible, and also to show you that the bass guitar and double bass are often a good "double" to have on a gig.

James Jamerson

Motown artist James Jamerson was rarely credited on that record company's hits of the 1960s, but his unusually melodic, improvisational style later brought him recognition as one of the most influential figures in the history of the bass guitar.

Biography

James Jamerson was born in Charleston, South Carolina in 1936, and moved to Detroit in 1954. He studied double bass at high school and started playing in the Detroit jazz clubs. He was offered a scholarship at Wayne State University, but turned it down in order to continue playing in the clubs. Shortly after this, he became the first-call bass player for many of the recording sessions in Detroit, where Motown was making its mark as a highly polished recording company. *(See also Motown, page 96.)*

Throughout 1959 and 1960, Jamerson recorded all of his Motown sessions on double bass, but he was given a Fender® Precision bass by Horace Ruth in 1961 and this soon became his main instrument. He played with all of the great Motown artists and on many of the hits, in particular on Marvin Gaye's *What's Going On* in 1971.

Jamerson died in Los Angeles in 1983.

Track 91

Bassline in the style of James Jamerson

James Jamerson, circa 1980, with his bass guitar

must know

Listen out for the genius of James Jamerson on bass with these artists in Motown recordings:
• Marvin Gaye's What's Going On
• Diana Ross & The Supremes
• The Four Tops
• The Temptations
• Martha Reeves & The Vandellas
• Gladys Knight & The Pips
• The above are available on compilations such as Motown: The Ultimate Collection (1998)

Style on bass

Jamerson took a great jazz technique from double bass across to the bass guitar. He insisted on a very high action on his Fender® Precision along with a set of LaBella flatwound strings. His jazz sensibility was demonstrated by the use of chromatic passing tones, raked notes and perfect time. His syncopated patterns with The Supremes, Four Tops, Marvin Gaye and The Temptations inspired many other players. Paul McCartney and John Paul Jones owe him a debt for his complex bass patterns.

Carol Kaye

Carol Kaye's recording credits include work, on both guitar and bass guitar, with The Beach Boys, The Monkees, Frank Zappa, Frank Sinatra, Ray Charles, Simon and Garfunkel, and Ike and Tina Turner. Her tutoring books have inspired many players.

Carol Kaye in the recording studio in 1973

Biography

Born into a musical family in 1935, Carol Kaye started playing bebop and backing many artists in LA clubs from the tender age of 14. She began her recording career backing Sam Cooke in 1957, and since then has played on thousands of sessions. In 1963, she moved to Fender® bass guitar after covering for another bass player in a Capitol Records session.

Carol began writing bass tutoring books in 1969. Her first title, *How to Play the Electric Bass*, effectively made the name of the Fender® bass synonymous with electric bass. Countless musicians around the world have followed her tips for playing and, in particular, for reading music on the bass. Carol Kaye has also played on many TV and film themes, including *Mission Impossible*, *MASH*, *Kojak*, *The Addams Family* and *The Cosby Show*.

Style on bass

Carol Kaye was one of the main American session players who developed the sound of the flat pick with flatwound strings on the bass guitar, or, more specifically, the Fender® Precision. This became the industry standard sound for many years because it gave record producers a clear bass sound with definition supplied by the slight 'click' of the pick.

Bassline in the style of Carol Kaye

Track 92

Previously the click was produced by adding another higher instrument, a muted baritone guitar, often called a 'tic-tac bass' in Nashville studios. This sound was also used in the 1960s by British session players, for example John Paul Jones, who applied the flat pick on flatwound strings on a Fender® Jazz bass on many pop recordings.

Paul McCartney

It goes without saying that The Beatles were one of the most influential bands of all time. McCartney has excelled in the triple roles of songwriter, singer and instrumentalist throughout his illustrious career; his mastery on bass is widely acknowledged.

**Bassline in the style of
Paul McCartney**

Track 93

must know

An excellent book about
the Beatles' recordings
is Revolution in the
Head, by Ian MacDonald
(Pimlico, 1997)

Biography

Paul McCartney was born in Walton, Liverpool, on 18th June, 1942. In 1953, he went to the Liverpool Institute, the town's top grammar school, where he met George Harrison. Paul was introduced to John Lennon at a church fete in July, 1957. John's band at the time was a skiffle group called The Quarry Men.

McCartney's early career with The Beatles involved visits to Hamburg, followed, in March 1961, by the first of many gigs at the Cavern Club in Liverpool. After several attempts by their manager, Brian Epstein, to secure a recording contract for them, in June 1962, they signed a contract to record demos for EMI producer, George Martin. The rest of the Beatles' story is history.

The Beatles broke up in 1970, and McCartney released his first solo album. A year later he formed Wings, which also had a string of hits.

McCartney has composed several pieces of classical music over the years, including the Liverpool Oratorio with Carl Davis. His involvement with avant garde art and electronic music since the 1960s is well documented in Barry Miles' book, *Many Years From Now*.

Paul McCartney was knighted in 1997.

Style on bass

Paul McCartney brought a melodic flair to the bass guitar that has been copied by many people but never matched. It is almost as if he and the other Beatles synthesized every style of popular music that they had ever heard – blues, R 'n' B, country, soul, Motown, girl-group, doo-wop and rock and roll – and from that created a completely fresh, new music. The Beatles' songs have inspired literally millions of people since the 1960s, and quite possibly will continue to do so for generations to come.

McCartney's bass playing was continually creative: compare the early stylings on *Love Me Do* (1962) and *Please Please Me* (1963), to sub-Stax riffs on *Drive My Car* (1965) and *Day Tripper* (1965; *see also Stax, page 97*), the psychedelic noodlings of *Come Together* (1969) and *Something* (1969), to the proto-thrash metal of *Helter Skelter* (1968).

must know
Paul McCartney plays bass on these albums:
• **With The Beatles:** Please Please Me, A Hard Day's Night, Beatles For Sale, Help!, Rubber Soul, Revolver, Sgt. Pepper's Lonely Hearts Club Band, Yellow Submarine, The White Album, Magical Mystery Tour, Abbey Road, Let It Be (all Parlophone)
• **With Wings:** Greatest Hits (Parlophone)

Paul McCartney with his Hohner bass guitar, circa 1965

Jack Bruce

Rock band Cream – consisting of Jack Bruce on bass and vocals, Eric Clapton on guitar and Ginger Baker on drums – played for only two years in the late 1960s. In that time, however, the band's creative hybrid of styles was hugely influential.

Biography

Jack Bruce was born in Glasgow on 14th May 1943. He studied cello and composition, then in 1962 joined Alexis Korner's Blues Inc., which was the first amplified R 'n' B band in Britain.

There is a great Blues Inc. recording of Jack Bruce on double bass, backing Cyril Davies singing *Hoochie Coochie Man*, and with Charlie Watts (later of the Rolling Stones) on drums.

Bruce then joined up with organist Graham Bond, drummer Ginger Baker and saxophonist Dick Heckstall-Smith to form the Graham Bond Organisation. It was during this period that Bruce was inspired to take up the bass guitar after hearing jazz bassist Roy Babbington play one. Bruce's first decent bass guitar was a Fender® Bass VI.

Bruce joined John Mayall's Bluesbreakers in 1965, in which he played bass alongside Eric Clapton's blues guitar. This was followed by a short spell with Manfred Mann. Then, in 1966, he joined together with Eric Clapton and Ginger Baker to form Cream.

Bruce changed to a Gibson EB-3 bass in Cream. He also wrote much of Cream's material and was the lead singer. The band quickly came to prominence with their ground-breaking hybrid of blues, jazz and psychadelic rock. Despite the acclaim and commer-

must know

Jack Bruce plays bass on the following:
- Alex Korner's Bootleg Him! (Castle, 1972)
- With Cream: Fresh Cream, Disraeli Gears, Wheels Of Fire, Goodbye (all Polydor, 1966–9)
- As soloist: Songs For A Tailor Polydor, 1969.
- Jack Harmony Row (Polydor)
- Tony Williams' Lifetime: Turn It Over (Verve, 1970)
- Frank Zappa: Apostrophe (Rykodisc, 1974)

Bassline in the style of Jack Bruce

Track 94

cial success, however, long-standing disagreements among band members led them to break up in 1968.

Since Cream, Bruce has had a successful solo career. He has also played with Tony Williams' band, Lifetime, and with Frank Zappa.

Style on bass

Jack Bruce's double bass playing is defined by three characteristics: a huge, bright tone; great timing; and excellent technique. This can be heard to great effect on the jazz album *Things We Like*, which he made with guitarist John McLaughlin in 1970.

Bruce transferred this amazing technique across to the bass guitar and came up with a style unique to him. With Cream, he combined the running counterpoint of Bach with bluesy slides, bends, and an almost BB King-type vibrato. Bruce and Ginger Baker have also acknowledged the influence of avant-garde jazz musicians Ornette Coleman and Charles Mingus when they were the powerhouse rhythm section of Cream.

Jack Bruce in the 1960s

Sting

A highly versatile composer, singer and musician, Sting became a household name in the late 1970s as the singer/bassist in The Police. The basslines on tracks by The Police have a certain reggae feel to them, but otherwise are hard to categorise.

Sting performing at a Police concert in Madison Square Garden, New York, in 2007

Biography

Sting, aka Gordon Sumner, was born in Newcastle upon Tyne in 1951. He started a career as a school teacher while playing guitar and bass guitar in his spare time. His first good bass was a second-hand Fender® Precision, and his early gigs were with such local bands as the Phoenix Jazzmen, Newcastle Big Band and Last Exit. It was from wearing a black and yellow stripey top while playing with the Phoenix Jazzmen that he first got his stage name, Sting.

Sting met drummer Stewart Copeland in 1976 and gave up his teaching job to focus on music. Copeland formed The Police in 1977, bringing Sting and guitarist Andy Summers on board.

Sting's solo career has been highly successful, too. He has recently recorded an album of John Dowland songs accompanied by lute.

Style on bass

Sting proved that it was possible to look like a punk, sing like an angel and play the bass guitar with panache. His punchy bass style locked in with the inspired reggae-style drum patterns of Stewart Copeland. Not only that, but his guitar playing was also cool enough for a tour (recorded on *Bring On The Night*, 1986) with Omar Hakim on drums (Weather

Report, Madonna), Darryl Jones on bass (Miles Davis, Rolling Stones) and Branford Marsalis on saxophone – sufficient tribute to Sting's all-round musicianship. His sparse basslines on such Police hits as *Roxanne*, *Can't Stand Losing You* and *So Lonely* are perfect examples of his precise style.

Bassline in the style of Sting with The Police

Track 95

must know

Sting plays bass on these recordings:
• With the Police: Outlandos D'Amour, Reggata De Blanc, Zenyatta Mondatta, Ghost In The Machine, Synchronicity
• Solo: The Dream Of The Blue Turtles, Acoustic Live In Newcastle, Bring On The Night, Brand New Day, All This Time

John Entwistle

His extraordinary style of bass in The Who brought John Entwistle
lasting fame as one of rock's most innovative artists. He also
designed his own hybrid Gibson Thunderbird bass with a
Fender® Precision neck, which he named the 'Fenderbird'.

**John Entwistle performing on a
TV show, circa 1967**

Biography

John Entwistle was born in Chiswick, London, in 1944.
He and his fellow school mates Pete Townshend and
Roger Daltrey formed The Who in 1964, with Keith
Moon later coming on board as drummer.

With The Who exploding onto the 60s music
scene, Entwistle experimented with increasingly
large amplifiers, eventually ending up with some of
the first bi-amped rigs for a fuller treble and bass
sound. Working with James Howe at Rotosound, he

developed the first roundwound bass guitar strings. Before this invention, bass guitarists had to peel off the black nylon coating on Rotosound TruBass strings to experiment with 'piano-string' tone. Entwistle also created the 'Fenderbird' and, in short, revolutionised the sound and style of rock bass playing.

Entwistle died of heart failure in 2002, one day before the planned start of a US tour with The Who.

Style on bass

Entwistle was highly creative with plectrum, fingerstyle and tapping, as well as using all four fingers to tap the strings percussively. Most of this experimentation was a way to keep up with Keith Moon's energetic technique on the drums.

His huge, trebly bass guitar sound at the beginning of *Substitute* (1966) and the distorted plectrum bass solo sections on *My Generation* (1965) were a wake up call to all bassists. An especially fine performance can be found on the *The Who: Live At Leeds* (1970). If you don't feel a rush of adrenaline while listening to the live version of *Shakin' All Over* or *Young Man Blues*, then you should probably think about taking up a more polite instrument, such as the flute.

Track 96

Bassline in the style of
John Entwistle

Paul Chambers

Rising to prominence in the 1950s, Paul Chambers was a master of jazz bass playing. All students of the bass guitar should listen to his skilful improvisations on double bass, which he played alongside Miles Davis and other big names in jazz.

Paul Chambers on his double bass in 1955

Biography

Paul Chambers was born in Pittsburgh, Pennsylvania in 1935. He moved to Detroit when he was 13, and studied baritone horn and tuba at school. He took up the double bass in 1949, and soon started playing in the clubs of Detroit. In 1955 he moved to New York while on tour with Paul Quinichette, and was accepted by all of the top players there.

Chambers played with the Miles Davis Quintet for eight years, and contributed on many sessions. He is the bass player on three of the best jazz albums of the late 50s and early 60s – Miles Davis' *Kind Of Blue*, John Coltrane's *Giant Steps* and Oliver Nelson's *The Blues And The Abstract Truth*. He died from TB in New York in January, 1969.

Style on bass

If you want to know about time, tone and note choice on bass, then listen to the four Miles Davis recordings on Prestige – *Cookin'*, *Steamin'*, *Workin'* and *Relaxin'* – and the best-selling jazz album of all time, *Kind Of Blue*. Paul Chambers' double bass style on these recordings provides enough fodder for a lifetime of study for any student of bass. If you have not tried to emulate at least one Paul Chambers bassline, then you cannot call yourself a bass player.

Track 97

must know

Paul Chambers plays bass on these and
other recordings:
• John Coltrane: Giant Steps (Atlantic, 1960)
• Miles Davis: Kind Of Blue (CBS/Sony, 1959)
• Oliver Nelson: The Blues and the
Abstract Truth (Impulse, 1961)

Charles Mingus

Throughout his career, Charles Mingus pushed the boundaries of jazz composition, combining gospel, blues, free jazz and elements of his musical idol, Duke Ellington.

Biography

Charles Mingus was born in Nogales, Arizona, in 1922, and raised in the Watts area of Los Angeles. At school he studied trombone and cello, and later took private tuition on double bass with jazz artist Red Callender and Herman Rheinschagen of the Philharmonic Orchestra. He also studied composition

must know

Recommended albums by Charles Mingus
• The Young Rebel (Properbox)
• Mingus Ah Um (CBS, 1959)
• East Coasting (WEA/Rhino, 1957)
• Oh Yeah! (Atlantic, 1961)
• Blues & Roots (Atlantic, 1960)
• Mingus Mingus Mingus Mingus Mingus (Impulse, 1963)

Charles Mingus on double bass in 1951

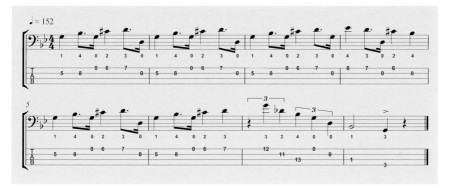

Bassline in the style of Charles Mingus

Track 98

with Lloyd Reese. In 1942 he played with Kid Ory and toured with Louis Armstrong and Lionel Hampton. However, it was not until 1950 that Mingus achieved national recognition with the Red Norvo Trio. Following this, he moved to New York and worked with Duke Ellington, Stan Getz, Bud Powell and Art Tatum. *Jazz At Massey Hall* (1953), with Charlie Parker and Dizzy Gillespie, was released on Mingus' own Debut label. He later wrote a quirky autobiography, *Beneath The Underdog*. He died in Mexico in 1979.

Style on bass

If you listen to *Mingus Fingers*, recorded with the Lionel Hampton Orchestra in 1947, followed by the 1963 masterpiece *Mingus Mingus Mingus Mingus Mingus*, you will see that Mingus maintained a high level of playing technique, creativity and sensitivity throughout his career. Then put on Jaco Pastorius' ground-breaking 1976 recording on bass guitar, *Jaco Pastorius*. You will be doubly inspired.

Flea

The bass guitarist of American alternative rock band Red Hot
Chili Peppers is a highly creative, energetic and experimental
musician, who has been playing instruments since childhood.

Biography

Flea was born Michael Peter Balzary in Melbourne,
Australia, in 1962. His family moved to New York in
1967, and then to Los Angeles in 1972. After
attending Fairfax High School in 1976, he joined the
Los Angeles Junior Philharmonic Orchestra on
trumpet. A friend at school, Hillel Slovak, later taught
Flea how to play bass, and they went on to form the

must know

Recommended
recordings by The Red
Hot Chili Peppers (all
with Capitol & Warner)
• The Red Hot Chili
Peppers
• Freakey Styley
• The Uplift Mofo
Party Plan
• Mother's Milk
• Blood Sugar Sex Magik
• One Hot Minute
• Californication
• By The Way
• Stadium Arcadium

**Flea in typically flamboyant outfit
playing with the Red Hot Chili
Peppers at Earl's Court in
London, 2006**

Red Hot Chili Peppers in 1983 from a group of friends at the same school.

As well as playing with the Chili Peppers, Flea has played bass and/or trumpet on sessions for Alanis Morissette, The Mars Volta, Nirvana and Ziggy Marley. He helped to set up the Silverlake Conservatory of Music in California, which offers tuition to young musicians who cannot afford lessons.

Bassline in the style of Flea

Track 99

Style on bass

Flea has taken the slap stylings of Larry Graham, Stanley Clarke and Bootsy Collins, together with a driven fingerstyle and a punk attitude to create one of the most distinctive bass sounds of the last 20 years. Dig out the Chili Peppers' version of Jimi Hendrix's *Fire* from *Mother's Milk* (1989) for a good example Flea's insistent fingerstyle playing. One of his most fluent slap basslines can be heard on *Aeroplane* from the 1995 album *One Hot Minute*.

11 Taking it further

In this section, we look at ways of taking your playing into different areas, such as trying out other bass instruments, and joining a band. We will also give you some useful tips about playing live gigs.

Other styles and ways of learning

We have covered the most popular bassline styles in this book, but there are many more world music styles that can provide inspiration for the bass player. We can also point you in the right direction if you want more advanced music tuition.

More world music styles

There are literally hundreds of world music styles to delve into; the styles listed below are merely a shortlist. The idea here is not to make your head spin with many new words and names, but to open up different sounds to you. In the 21st century we have access to much of the music written from the 12th century (Hildegard of Bingen and such composers) to the present day. We should, at least, be guided to listen to, and absorb, as much of this music as we are able. Don't be blinkered and trapped into thinking that there is only one style of music for you. All such music styles need some sort of bass instrument.

Recommended for further listening:
• Balkans: some styles are notable for odd time signatures, especially Bulgarian wedding music
• China: various traditional zither and lute music
• Congo: *soukous* (sometimes called African rumba) – acoustic bass, drums and brass instruments
• Ghana and Nigeria: highlife – fusion of African and Western styles with guitars, drums and brass
• India: classical *raga* melodies and modern music
• Indonesia: traditional Javanese and Balinese *gamelan* music

- Mali and Guinea: *griot* (praise singing), *kora* (a lute-like instrument) and *balafon* (percussion) music
- Mongolia: vocal traditions
- Portugal: *fado* (singing and Portuguese guitar)
- Senegal and Gambia: the *griot* tradition, especially Youssou N'Dour
- South Africa: jazz, pop, and traditional Zulu music
- Spain: flamenco, in particular Carles Benavent with Paco de Lucia
- Vietnam: traditional and modern, especially the French-Vietnamese jazz musician Nguyên Lê

Personal tuition

John Lennon, Paul McCartney, Eric Clapton and Mark Knopfler all started their musical self-tuition with a copy of Bert Weedon's *Play In A Day* book. Using this *Need To Know* book and practising every day will take you down the road to competence on the bass guitar within a few months.

If you want to advance your knowledge and technique further, the best step is to find a good teacher. If you have a music shop near you, then ask them for recommended teachers, or check on their notice-board. Look up music colleges that offer electric guitar, bass guitar and drums (these instruments are largely ignored by the classical music colleges). The leading schools of contemporary music are often at the forefront of academia, with many students gaining degrees and entering the music business professionally.

Other bass instruments

Once you have learnt to play the four-string bass guitar, there are several other related instruments that you might want to consider adding to your musical armoury.

A five-string bass guitar - the extra string being the thick, low B

Basses with more than four strings

The five- and six-stringed bass guitars are probably the most obvious options that will be of interest to players who have gained experience on the four-string bass guitar.

A five-string bass with a low B string will give you access to the same range as some of the synth basslines that have been common for many years. The thing to watch out for, when first playing one of these instruments, is the affliction of 'five-string fumble'. This occurs when you play a phrase, or riff, a fourth lower than usual because you think that the B string is actually your E string.

Some players will put a high C string onto their five-string bass to give more range in the higher register. Following on from this, the six-string bass with both low B and high C strings gives you the best of both worlds. However, the extra range in both directions can be just too much temptation for some people. A word of advice: only take a six-string bass to gigs that actually require one. Otherwise, the other players in the band – i.e. guitarists – may be worried that you are going to stray into their territory...

Fretless bass guitars

Another option would be to get hold of a fretless bass guitar. Many players now go for the fretless J-bass to try to emulate the sound of Jaco Pastorius with roundwound strings. There are other fretless instruments that sound good, such as the P-bass. You might even want to consider having the frets taken out of a fretted bass – with this purpose in mind, you could buy one that is identical to the fretted bass you play already. Some players now use flatwound strings on a fretless bass guitar to obtain a more portable double bass-type sound.

The double bass

Which brings us to the double bass. The author would strongly recommend any bass guitarist to also learn how to play the double bass, or at the very least to listen to the double bass for inspiration. Double bass is a very good double for the bass guitar, as well as being a very satisfying instrument to play. If your home does not have room for a full-bodied acoustic bass, then an upright electric bass would be another good option.

must know

There are many other bass options. The nearest one to the bass guitar in common use is the tuba, or sousaphone. (OK, it doesn't have strings, but it makes a great sound.) You could also equip yourself with a small, portable synthesizer on which to play basslines. Being able to play a keyboard adds to your employ-ability too.

Playing with a band

You might already be in a band, perhaps with a bunch of friends, and playing mainly for your own enjoyment in someone's house. Or perhaps you are looking to join a band and/or start playing proper gigs. We've got some essential tips on these subjects.

Joining a band

The most obvious route to joining a band is to get together with your friends or colleagues. If you have a pool of people who are keen to play music, then use it. If you need to search further afield, then the noticeboard of a music shop may prove helpful. *NME* has a board on its website (www.nme.com) for bands in the UK who are looking for new members. And if you take a course at a top music college, then you are bound to meet fellow musicians interested in forming a band.

When you audition to be in a band, think about how to project yourself. If the advert says 'Bass player wanted for Jam tribute band', then you might want to

Rock band in performance

kit yourself out with a black suit and thin tie, and a Rickenbacker bass. If the ad says 'Bassist wanted for punk band', do not turn up with a six-string bass.

Playing gigs

There are many ways in which you can start playing gigs. Pubs offering live music nights are always on the lookout for up-and-coming bands. You will probably need to go and demonstrate your skills to the landlord or audition for some venues.

You will have to deal with a variety of people, so it's handy if at least one band member has good liaison skills. In fact, the bass player is usually the diplomat in the band – the one who has to smooth over any wrinkles that may occur among band members, and promoters, agents and fixers.

Always make sure that you turn up on time for a gig; if possible, be early. The quickest way to get a bad reputation is to be always late. And keep the ingestion of liquid stimulants to a minimum. That is, don't get drunk before your big gig. This is easier said than done, particularly if you are nervous. But you really won't play well if you are drunk, and you won't be able to drive the equipment back home, either.

Here is another tip: on any gig there will always, without fail, be a 'jobsworth' who will tell you: a) you cannot park your car there; b) you cannot bring your equipment in that way; c) you cannot do something else, which you hadn't imagined would be important when you decided to become a musician, but it will keep you from setting up for the gig.

The safest thing in such situations is to smile sweetly and, if possible, ignore the jobsworth (though not if it means your car getting clamped).

must know

Checklist of equipment to take to a gig:
• **Bass guitar (musicians have been known to take everything except their actual instrument!)**
• **Stand for instrument**
• **Jack-to-jack lead, plus a spare**
• **Amplifier – have it PAT-tested by a competent electrician**
• **Spare strings**
• **Extension power cable**
• **Bass D.I. box to connect to a P.A. system**
• **Tuner – check battery and take a spare**
• **Music stand if it is a reading gig**
• **Music notation**
• **Suitable clothing**
• **Address, map, directions**
• **Change for parking meter**

When you have arrived at the gig, loaded all of your gear into the venue, parked the car, set up your equipment, tuned your bass and done the sound check, then you are ready to do what you have spent ages preparing for. That is, play live music to an enthusiastic and appreciative audience, we hope...

Hand signals for the band

Imagine this scenario. The guitarist in your band is frantically trying to find out what key the next tune is in. You shout *"B flat!"* across the noisy pub stage while your drummer practises his latest lick at a volume guaranteed to punch holes in brick walls. Of course, your guitar-playing friend starts the next song in E flat because – although he is extremely talented – lip reading is not one of his skills.

What you and your band need to learn is the system of hand signals that most professional musicians recognise.

Form a letter C with your thumb and forefinger – this indicates that the next tune you're going to play will be in the key of C major.

Fingers held down indicate flats. The code is one finger for F, two for B♭, three for E♭. Similarly, fingers held up indicate sharp keys – one for G, two for D, three for A. This is usually up to a maximum of five fingers using one hand (six and seven become a bit too ungainly).

Health warning – while these hand signals can be very useful, the author cannot be held responsible for any misunderstandings that might arise from their misuse!

must know

A good way to build up contacts within the music industry – including promoters, agents and record companies – is to join, in the UK, the Musicians' Union, or in the USA, the American Federation of Musicians, also known as the Musicians' Union.
• www.musiciansunion.org.uk
• www.afm.org

When you hit a wrong note

Hopefully, you will already have done many rehearsals with your band, and your knowledge of the music and all of the arrangements will be encyclopaedic. However, whether you are playing with written music or from memory, and even if you are an excellent player, you will sometimes make a mistake when playing live.

The best piece of advice in such situations – if you make what jazz players call a 'clam' – is to act as if nothing has happened. Do not attempt to apologise, or pull a face, or signal in any way that something bad has happened.

Recording your own music

In the recording studio, by contrast, you have the freedom to go over a piece of music again and again until it is as perfect as possible.

You don't necessarily need access to a professional recording studio. A music recording outfit can be set up quite easily in the home using a desktop or laptop computer with sequencing software such as Pro Tools, Logic or Cubase. The author uses Logic software on a MacBook to record riffs and melodies – the connection is made from the bass guitar using a 'Monster' jack-to-stereo mini-jack plugged directly into the audio output of the laptop. The sound quality can be surprisingly good for the money.

You and your band can record yourselves playing together, or individually, and use samples from various sources to mix together on the computer. You can then burn your own music tracks onto CDs.

Glossary

I, II, III, IV, V, VI, VII (Roman numerals) Conventional way of labelling the seven degrees of the harmonised major scale, and their corresponding triad chords.

4/4 Four-beat rhythm.

accidental Sign for a temporary sharp, flat or natural.

acoustic bass Non-electric bass instruments, most commonly now applied to the double bass.

amplifier A device which converts the signal from your bass into sound via a loudspeaker.

arpeggio Four-note chords that are played in quick succession rather than sounded together.

augmented Sharpened interval; raised by a semitone.

bar In musical notation, a segment or measure with a given number of beats, denoted with a vertical line on the stave.

bass The lowest part of a piece of music.

bass clef Symbol at beginning of stave indicating bass pitch.

bassline Musical phrase for a bass.

beat Rhythmic pulse.

blues scale Scale that uses 'blue notes'.

bpm Beats per minute.

bridge Part on bass over which the strings pass to a tailpiece.

chord Several notes at given intervals played in succession or together.

chord progression Sequence of chords.

chromatic Relating to a sequence of semitones.

clef Symbol indicating pitch of the notes.

combo A combination amplifier and speaker box.

contrabass Another name for double bass.

crotchet See quarter note.

cut common time Form of notation used in older jazz styles.

cycle of fourths/fifths Diagram that helps musicians work out and memorise the order of key signatures.

D.C. 'Da Capo' on notation, means to go back and repeat the whole thing.

dead note A note that is not sounded out in full.

degree Step of a scale.

diminished Flattened interval; lowered by a semitone.

double bass Large fretless stringed instrument used in classical orchestras and jazz.

eighth note (quaver) Note that is one-eighth of a whole note – represents half a beat in 4/4 time.

Fender® bass Bass instrument made by Fender®.

fingerboard Part of bass where contact is made by the fingers pressing down on the strings.

fingering pattern In this book, the numbers directly below the stave suggest which fingers to use *(see p.34).*

finger-per-fret system Using four fingers to cover four frets at a time.

fingerstyle Plucking the strings with your fingertips.

flat ♭ Note that is one semitone lower.

frets Raised strips across the neck of the bass, indicating where notes should be played. They are counted down from the headstock on the bass.

fretless Instrument without frets.

Gibson Manufacturer.

groove Rhythmic feel to a piece of popular music.

half note (minim) Note that is half of a whole note – represents two beats in 4/4 time.

harmonic minor scale Minor scale with a raised seventh degree.

harmonics In acoustics theory, wave frequencies that have algebraically constant relationships with each other and sound pleasant to the human ear.

harmonised major scale A scale in which the notes of the major scale have been taken as the root notes for a series of triad chords.

headstock End of bass where the strings are usually attached to the machine heads.

improvisation Usually means playing a new tune over a given set of chords.

interval Distance in pitch between two notes *(see p.107).*

intonation A form of tuning.

inversion Series of notes inverted from a parent chord, e.g. first inversion from third of chord.

Jazz bass (J-bass) Trademark of Fender® for their bass model with two separate, single-coil pickups. Is often used as a generic term.

key Tonality; pertaining to a specific scale.

key signature Number of sharps or flats in a key.

ledger lines Extra lines above or below a stave to extend the range of notes that can be shown.

legato Performed with a smooth connection between the notes.

luthier Someone who builds and repairs guitars and basses.

machine head Mechanism for raising or lowering the pitch of strings in tuning (sometimes mistakenly referred to as tuning pegs, which is the guitar term).

major scale Commonly used scale, also called Ionian mode.

melodic minor scale Minor scale with major sixth and major seventh degrees.

metronome Device giving tempo.

minim *See* half note.

minor scale Commonly used scale, also called Aeolian mode.

modes Musical variations based on the steps of the major scale.

natural Not sharp or flat.

neck Long part of the bass where most notes are played.

neck diagram A diagram showing where fingers go on the neck (chapter 5).

notation A stave with notes and other musical symbols marked *(see p.48).*

nut Place where the strings sit at the top of the neck of the bass guitar.

octave Interval between two notes of the same name.

open string A string played without being stopped anywhere on the neck.

pentatonic scale Scale with five notes.

perfect Class of interval.

phrase A short musical expression.

pick/plectrum Triangular shaped device for plucking strings.

pickup Device that converts the vibrations from the strings into an electric signal.

pitch Frequency, or height, of a note.

plucking Fingerstyle.

position (fret) markers Dots on the bass neck that help you find the right fret. Single dots appear before the 3rd, 5th, 7th, 9th, 15th, 17th and 19th frets. A pair of dots marks the octave at the 12th.

Precision (P-bass) Brand of bass made by Fender®.

quarter note (crotchet) Note that is one-quarter of a whole note – represents one beat in 4/4 time.

quaver *See* eighth note.

raking the action of dragging one finger across several strings.

rehearsal letter In notation, denotes a change, such as where a chorus begins.

rest symbol denoting an interval of silence.

rhythm General pattern of a piece of music.

Rickenbacker Manufacturer.

riff Repeated phrase.

root note First note of a scale or chord.

scales Ladder-like sequences of notes.

score Notation for a full piece of music.

scratchplate A piece of plastic to protect the bass body from scratches.

semibreve *See* whole note.

semiquaver *See* sixteenth note.

semitone A half-step interval in pitch, equal to one fret on the bass guitar.

sharp Note that is one semitone higher.

signature Information about time and key at beginning of the stave.

sixteenth note (semiquaver) Note that is one-sixteenth of a whole note – represents a quarter of a beat in 4/4 time.

skip Shortened note within a walking bassline.

slapping Playing technique on bass *(see p.40).*

Squier Bass manufacturer.

stab phrasing A chord played with force.

staccato Shortening symbol.

stave In musical notation, the grid of five lines and four spaces onto which notes and other musical symbols are written.

stopped note A note played on a string that is 'stopped' by a finger at some point along the neck of the instrument.

Stratocaster Brand of electric guitar made by Fender®.

string bass Another name for the double bass.

string crossing Moving from one string to another in a scalar passage.

strings Usually made of stainless steel or nickel/steel on a bass guitar.

stroking Using the fleshy part of the fingertips, rather than plucking.

swing rhythm/swung notes Rhythm using a triplet subdivision of the beat.

syncopated rhythm Emphasised off-beats, much used in jazz.

tablature Diagrams for beginners that suggest which frets can be used to play notes *(see p.50)*.

Telecaster Brand of electric guitar made by Fender®.

tempo Speed of a piece of music.

tetrachord Four-note pattern of tones.

ties/tied notes Notes on the stave connected by a curved line.

time signature Piece of information about time at beginning of the stave – the top number shows the number of beats in a bar; the bottom number shows what kind of note. The most common time signature is 4/4.

tone Timbre; interval of two semitones.

triad Three-note shape at given intervals.

triplet Group of three notes subdividing a beat.

truss rod Metal rod inside neck of the bass guitar, which stops the neck from bowing from the pressure of the strings.

tuner Electronic device that aids in the process of tuning an instrument to a reference pitch or note.

tuning Process of adjusting the pitch of an instrument so that it is identical to a reference pitch.

tuning peg *See* machine head.

tuning post Part of bass into which the ends of the strings are inserted and wrapped around.

two-feel When a piece of music is counted in four, but the bass and drums play in two with the half note, rather than the quarter note as the pulse.

unison Two notes of the same pitch.

upright bass Another name for double bass.

walking bassline A steady, even rhythm that 'walks' smoothly through chord changes – used in jazz and some other music styles.

whole note (semibreve) A full note – represents a whole bar in 4/4.

Index

Further reading and listening

Bibliography

Aebersold, Jamey: *Charlie Parker Omnibook –
Bass Clef*, Atlantic, 1978

Bellson, Louis: *Modern Reading Text in 4/4*,
Belwin Mills, 1963

Brown, Ray: *Bass Method*, Hal Leonard, 1999

Dean, Dan: *Electric Bass Composite (Books 1, 2
& 3)*, Hal Leonard, 1996

Goldsby, John, et al: *Ron Carter Bass Lines To Vol
6 'All Bird'*, Aebersold, 1979

Goldsby, John: *The Jazz Bass Book*, Backbeat,
2002

Hodgkinson, Colin: *Bass Master*, KDM (not for
beginners) 2000

Kaye, Carol: *Electric Bass Lines Complete (Vols 1
& 2)*, Alfred, 1986

Levine, Mark: *The Jazz Theory Book*, Sher Music,
1995

del Puerto, Carlos: *The True Cuban Bass*, Sher
Music, 1994

Rainey, Chuck: *The Complete Electric Bass
Player – Books 1, 2, 3 & 4*, Amsco

The Real Book – Bass Clef, Wise/Hal Leonard,
2006

Richmond, Mike: *Modern Walking Bass
Technique*, Ped Xing Music, 1983

Roberts, Jim: *How The Fender Bass Changed The
World*, Backbeat, 2001

Sher, Chuck: *The New Real Book – Vols 1, 2 & 3*,
Sher Music, 1988

Sher, Chuck: *The Real Easy Book – Bass Clef*,
Sher Music, 2003

Slutsky, Allan: *Standing in the Shadows of
Motown*, Hal Leonard, 1988

Slutsky, Allan: *The Great James Brown Rhythm
Sections*, Warner, 1997

Westwood, Paul: *Bass Bible*, Ama Verlag, 2001

Willis, Gary: *Ultimate Ear Training For Guitar &
Bass*, Hal Leonard, 1998

Discography

Allman Brothers Band: *Legendary Hits*,
Polygram, 1994

Back Door: *Back Door*, Warner Bros, 1973;
8th Street Nites, 1973

Beach Boys: *Summer Dreams*,
Capitol, 1990

Berlin, Jeff: *Taking Notes*, Denon, 1997

Black Sabbath: *Black Sabbath*, Vertigo, 1970;
Paranoid, 1970

Black Uhuru: *The Dub Factor*, Spectrum, 1983

Bond, Graham: *Sound Of '65*, BGO, 1965;
There's a Bond Between Us, 1999

Clarke, Stanley: *School Days*, Epic, 1976

Cream: *Fresh Cream*, Polydor, 1966; *Disraeli
Gears*, 1967; *Wheels Of Fire*, 1968; *Goodbye*,
Polydor, 1969

Davis, Miles: *Kind Of Blue*, CBS/Sony, 1959

Deep Purple: *Deep Purple In Rock*, EMI, 1970;
Machine Head, EMI, 1972

Ellington, Duke: *In A Mellotone*, RCA/BMG,
1957; *The Jimmy Blanton Era 1939-41*, *Giants
Of Jazz*, 1990

Fagen, Donald: *The Nightfly*, Warner, 1982

Fairport Convention: *Liege & Lief*, Island, 1969

Fleetwood Mac: *The Best Of*, Columbia, 1996

Ford, Robben: *Talk To Your Daughter*, Warner
Bros, 1988

Free: *The Free Story*, Island, 1973

Graham, Larry: *The Best Of Larry Graham* and
Graham Central Station, Warner, 1996

Hendrix, Jimi: *Are You Experienced?*,
Polydor/MCA, 1967; *Axis: Bold As Love*, 1967;
Electric Ladyland, 1968

Hodgkinson, Colin: *The Bottom Line: Bass Solos And Trios*, InAkustik, 1998

Karr, Gary: *JS Bach Solo Suites*, Amati, 2005

King, Albert: *Born Under A Bad Sign*, Stax, 1967

King, BB: *Live At The Regal*, MCA, 1964 & 1997

King, Freddy: *Blues Guitar Hero*, Federal / Ace, 1993

Led Zeppelin: *Led Zeppelin I*, Atlantic, 1969; *Led Zeppelin II*, 1969; *Led Zeppelin III*, 1970; *Led Zeppelin IV*, 1971

Marley, Bob: *Legend*, Island, 1984

The Mars Volta: *De-Loused In The Comatorium*, Universal, 2003; *Frances The Mute*, 2005

Mayall, John: *Bluesbreakers With Eric Clapton*, Decca, 1966 & 1998

Mingus, Charles: *Mingus Ah Um*, CBS, 1959; *East Coasting*, WEA/Rhino, 1957; *Oh Yeah!*, Atlantic, 1961; *Blues & Roots*, Atlantic, 1960; *Mingus Mingus Mingus Mingus Mingus*, Impulse, 1963

Mitchell, Joni: *Mingus*, Asylum, 1979

Nelson, Oliver: *The Blues And The Abstract Truth*, Impulse, 1961

Pastorius, Jaco: *Metheny Bley Ditmas – Jaco*, Jazz Door, 1974; *Jaco Pastorius*, Epic, 1976

Pentangle: *Light Flight*, Recall, 1997

Pettiford, Oscar: *Lucky Thompson Meets Oscar Pettiford*, Fresh Sound, 2006

The Police: *The Police*, Polydor, 2007

Presley, Elvis: *The Collection*, Vol 1, RCA/BMG, 1984; *Sunrise*, 1999

The Rolling Stones: *The London Years*, London

Santana, Carlos: *Abraxas*, CBS, 1970

Sun Records: *The Legendary Sun Records Story*, Castle, 2000

Tool: *Aenima*, Volcano, 1996; *Lateralus*, 2001

Weather Report: *Heavy Weather*, Columbia, 1977; *Domino Theory*, 1984

The Who: *Live At Leeds*, Polydor, 1970 & 1995

Wonder, Stevie: *Songs in the Key Of Life*, Motown, 1976; *Hotter Than July*, 1980

Yes: *Fragile*, Atlantic, 1972

Zappa, Frank: *Uncle Meat*, Rykodisc, 1968; *Tinseltown Rebellion*, Rykodisc, 1981

Webography

Institute of Contemporary Music Performance: www.icmp.uk.com

The Gallery: www.thebassgallery.com

Overwater Bass Emporium: www.overwater.co.uk

Guitar Emporium: www.guitaremporium.co.uk

The Bass Centre: www.basscentre.com

Carol Kaye: www.carolkaye.com

NME band message board: www.nme.com

CD track listing

ACKNOWLEDGEMENTS

About the author

Paul Scott is a leading educationalist who teaches at The Institute Of Contemporary Music Performance (formerly Guitar Institute and Basstech) in London, the University of East London and Thames Valley University. He is a Fellow of the Higher Education Academy (FHEA). He studied double bass with Gary Karr and Bronwen Naish, and has played double bass and bass guitar professionally since the mid-1970s. He was Music Editor of *Bassist* magazine from 1994 to 2000.

The author would like to thank these people:
Jason How at Rotosound strings; all at ICMP; Carol Kaye for all of her help with this book and over the years; all of my teachers, in particular, Bronwen Naish and Gary Karr; and all of my students.

Musical arrangements: Paul Scott
CD recording: Iain Scott

Studio photography, design and editorial:
Thameside Media Projects
www.thamesidemedia.com

Photographer: Mike Ellis
Models: Conrad Bell, Ida Brox, Lee Feltham, Paul Scott, Carolina Shamshoum, Daniel Szymczak, Christine Weir

Picture credits:
Image on p.152 & 156 by courtesy of Carol Kaye.
Images on p.155, 159, 161, 162, 164, 166, 168, 170 by courtesy of Getty Images.
Images on p.13, 16, 17, 176, 178 by courtesy of iStockPhoto.com.
All other images by Thameside Media Projects.

:C: **Collins** need to know?

Look out for these recent titles in Collins' practical and accessible need to know? series.

Other titles in the series:

**To order any of these titles, please telephone 0870 787 1732 quoting reference 263H.
For further information about all Collins books, visit our website: www.collins.co.uk**